An Illustrated History of
MIDLAND WAGONS

by R. J. Essery

Volume One

Oxford Publishing Co.

First published 1979
Reprinted 1984
This impression 1998

ISBN 0 86093 040 8

Published by Oxford Publishing Co

an imprint of Ian Allan Publishing Ltd, Terminal House, Station Approach, Shepperton, Surrey TW17 8AS.
Printed by WBC Book Manufacturers Ltd, Waterton Industrial Estate, Bridgend, Mid Glamorgan CF31 3XP.

Title page

Two Midland Railway class 3, 0-6-0s hauling a wartime train of shells for the army in France seen here passing Attenborough on the 17th September, 1916.

Photograph Courtesy
British Rail and the
National Railway Museum

INTRODUCTION

"The Midland was a magnificent Railway" wrote C. Hamilton Ellis in his book *The Midland Railway* published by Ian Allan Ltd. in 1953. Regrettably, the author recorded little of its freight stock.

In track mileage, the Midland was third only to the GWR and the L&NWR, and the position of the L&NWR in this league table was further strengthened by the merging with the L&YR. However, in terms of freight stock owned, it was the Premier Company. According to the 1922 Railway Year Book, the North Eastern Railway freight and service stock numbered 126,484 vehicles. The Midland Railway owned 123,429 plus 2,621 NCC, 50% of the SDJR's stock of 229, 50% of M & GN stock (which totalled 388), one-third CLC stock whose total reached 4,510 and 50% of the 312 vehicles belonging to the CDJC: a grand total of 128,017.

To date, there have been several histories of the Midland, by E. G. Barnes, C. Hamilton Ellis, Clement Stretton, F. S. Williams and a much more recent production by George Dow, F.R.S.A., F.C.I.T., President of the Historical Model Railway Society has dealt with liveries and associated subjects. However, the very scope of the subject of freight stock prevented any author from doing more than providing enthusiasts with an appetizer for this aspect of Midland affairs.

Railway enthusiasts in general and modellers, to whom this book is directed, demand accuracy and, whilst I do not claim to have produced the definitive work, at least I have tried to provide more information about Midland wagons than has appeared to date. There are omissions, the passage of time and lack of early records make this a certain fact; that there are errors, is probably also true, but these errors are the author's responsibility alone. In producing a work of this nature, it is impossible for one person alone to undertake the task and the author has been fortunate in being able to call upon a number of his friends to assist in the task and it is only appropriate that their names should be recorded in alphabetical order. To these gentlemen may I express my grateful thanks.

T.W. Bourne, H.C. Casserley, P.G. Chatham, R. Chorley, C. Crofts, George Dow, T.J. Edgington, A.G. Ellis, G.K. Fox, M.D. Hart, G.N.I. Ibbott, D. Jenkinson, R.E. Lacy, D. Larkin, E.G. Mackenzie, K.R. Morgan, M. Peascod, C.M. Stevens, T.W. Shuttleworth, P. Tatlow, A.E. West, A. Whitehead, R.E. Wilson, K.C. Woodhead.

My thanks also to Mrs. Marlane Parker and Mrs. Sylvia Wall who patiently translated my scrawl into a typed manuscript for the publisher.

Finally, my grateful appreciation to my publisher, who allowed me to write his first two volume work dealing with freight stock.

AUTHOR'S NOTES

I was particularly pleased to learn that following the acquisition of the OPC imprint, Ian Allan planned to reprint *Midland Wagons*. These volumes; researched during the late 1960s and early 1970s, were published many years ago and have been out of print for a long time. It all began as a joint project with my dear friend, the late Bill Steel, but following his untimely death I was able to continue using a copy of the Lot list, a handful of general arrangement drawings, a copy of the wagon diagram book to complete the work. Thus *Midland Wagons* became my first title written as the sole author.

During the past few years new material has become available which has enabled me to expand upon the content of *Midland Wagons* and, to confirm that, by and large, the original research was sound. This new material included a considerable number of general arrangement and detail drawings, some new photographs hitherto unpublished, and the carriage & wagon department drawing register for the years 1873-1926. This valuable document, now held at the NRM, York, together with the drawings, and additional copies of wagon diagrams books has enabled me to expand on my original work.

The introduction of *Midland Record*, an occasional journal published by Wild Swan Publications Ltd, provided the opportunity to make this new material available to readers interested in the story of the Midland Railway's wagon stock. During the past few years a number of articles have been published where it was possible to go into greater detail about specific vehicles, using new material thereby expanding upon the content to be found in *Midland Wagons*. Towards the end of 1998, a *Midland Record* supplement dealing with a number of different wagon designs will be pub-

lished, but in every case, the core reference is the original research published in *Midland Wagons*.

Therefore readers can be assured that *Midland Wagons* provides a sound grounding into the subject but further information has, and will continue to be published in various issues of *Midland Record*.

Bob Essery, Rolleston-on-Dove, Staffs, 1998

Two Midland 0-6-0s in LMS ownership hauling a freight train. Unfortunately the location and engine numbers are unknown.

Author's Collection

CONTENTS

◁ **Plate 1** This wonderful view of Derby contains a wealth of interest from the carriages on the extreme left and the old Kirtley goods brake van featured again in Chapter Eleven, to the dumb buffered ex private owner coal wagons in Midland Railway ownership. In addition, there are numerous examples of early low goods wagons and the narrow bodies with wider headstocks which can be clearly seen.

The numbers of the locomotives are not known.

British Rail

Plate 2 A Midland goods train in the last years of the nineteenth century hauled by a Kirtley 0-6-0 No. 864. Apart from this being a particularly delightful photograph, the author was interested in the first vehicle—an example of an early 6-ton lowside goods wagon. The other two wagons visible are ex private owner coal wagons, purchased by the Midland and running in Midland Railway livery.

British Rail

Plate 2

Above
Class 3, 0-6-0, No. 3258 hauling a mineral train on Hathern Troughs
on July 19th, 1911.

Below
Class 3, 0-6-0Ts, Nos. 1930 and 1939 banking a northbound frei
train on the Lickey Incline on 30th April, 1920.

Both photographs National Railway Muse

Chapter 1 General Introduction

The Midland Railway had presence. By 1923, it extended from Shoeburyness to Carlisle and from Lincoln to Bath and Bristol. Detached from the main body of the system in England were lines in Wales, Ireland and jointly owned in Scotland—a feat equalled only by the London & North Western.

During the 79 years of its existence, it became one of the best railways in Great Britain in the services it provided to the travelling public, with its splendid main lines and clean and efficient stations. The Midland pioneered the system of centralised traffic control and its influence after 1923, when it became part of the LMS, scarcely diminished for several years. Midland livery was the basis of that adopted by the newly formed Company for the locomotive, carriage and wagon fleets and Midland design practices continued almost undiluted across almost the whole spectrum of the early LMS scene.

In the realm of freight stock, the Midland hardly paused in 1923 and, by 1924, new construction, with one or two minor exceptions, was either to Midland designs, standardised by the new enlarged Company, or new LMS designs based firmly upon Midland practice. Midland methods of recording wagons by diagram continued and a new series of lot numbers commenced. Thus, as with many other aspects of the early LMS, freight stock too became yet another outward manifestation of the "Greater Midland".

However, the early years of the Midland in terms of freight stock, can be likened to the dark ages of English history—indeed the period from 1843 until 1877 contains very little solid information, compared with the period from 1877 to 1923 and there are several reasons for this lack of information. Early construction was hardly recorded in the works and it was ignored by photographers and writers. This is not surprising, since it is only in recent years that freight stock has even begun to achieve any degree of general recognition; yet, on most lines in this country, the revenue from freight greatly exceeded that from passengers.

Since this early period is, as it were, lost in the "mists of antiquity", the basis for this work has been perforce the lot book, begun at Derby following the opening of the new works in 1877. This invaluable document, together with photographs from private and official sources, coupled with a diagram book and some original general arrangement drawings, has enabled this pictorial history to be written. Therefore, some preliminary remarks regarding this source material would not be out of place at this juncture.

The dates quoted in the lot book and repeated in the main body of the text are the dates that construction was authorised, and it is possible that, in many instances, the vehicles concerned did not appear until the following year. The official drawings do not always indicate what was built. As will be seen, the Midland was quite capable of taking a drawing of a covered goods wagon and building it 6" or 12" higher or building a cattle wagon 3" longer to the "same" specification.

The diagram book was only issued during the latter period of the Company's history, and even this was not complete in that some stock was not included and no attempt was made to cover the detail variations beloved by modellers. Diagrams were for internal use and it was the basic dimensions which mattered. However, within the constraints of the above, it is hoped that the treatment of the subject will meet with most readers' approval.

A copy of all the diagrams in the last Midland diagram book has been included within this work and all copies have been reduced to 4 mm scale. In addition, certain other drawings produced by well known modellers have been included to either 4 mm or 7 mm scale, so that greater detail can be recorded. To a certain extent, these drawings duplicate the diagrams but it was felt that the historical value of the diagrams was such that they should all be featured and they are listed overleaf. The only alteration on this 'Index of Wagons' has been to include the relevant chapters where they appear because, rather than follow the original Midland sequence, the author has developed chapters around various types of vehicles and allocated the diagrams accordingly. Some pre-diagram stock appears within the later chapters but the majority of early stock built before 1877 will be found in Chapter One.

Overleaf is the copy of the most up to date version of the index of Midland Wagon Stock and careful study will reveal a number of discrepancies. For example, the covered goods vans in the index are often described as "covered goods wagons" on the diagrams and other minor variations occur.

The gaps in the diagram numbers were probably to allow for new construction and an earlier version has gaps which were later filled while a later version has had one of the early covered goods wagon pages removed.

The Midland page number, description and diagram number have been accurately reproduced but the Fig. No. and page numbers refer to their location within these present volumes. Finally, it should be noted that the final construction did not enjoy a diagram number or perhaps it would be more accurate to state that it is believed they were not allocated a diagram number. The author has been unable to trace them and reference to these vehicles is mentioned in the relevant chapters.

INDEX OF MIDLAND WAGON STOCK

MR Page No.	Description	Diagram	Fig. No.	Page	Volume
81	25 Ton Timber Truck	D827	163	—	Vol. 2
82	35 Ton Machinery Trolley	D1095	164	—	Vol. 2
83	50 Ton Armour Plate Wagon	D782	165	—	Vol. 2
84	40 Ton Armour Plate Wagon	D328	166	—	Vol. 2
85	30 Ton Bogie Rail Truck	D330	167	—	Vol. 2
86	35 Ton Bogie Rail Truck	D340	168	—	Vol. 2
87	15 Ton Bogie Tramcar Truck	D318	169	—	Vol. 2
90	15 Ton Trolley	D311	127	—	Vol. 2
91	18 Ton Trolley	D310	128	—	Vol. 2
92	18 Ton Trolley (Steel frame)	D653	129	—	Vol. 2
93	25 Ton Trolley	D642	170	—	Vol. 2
94	30 Ton Trolley	D309	175	—	Vol. 2
95	35 Ton Trolley	D702	176	—	Vol. 2
96	40 Ton Trolley	D308	177	—	Vol. 2
97	60 Ton Trolley	D693	178	—	Vol. 2
98	8 Ton Circular Plate Wagon	D322	130	—	Vol. 2
99	5 Ton Deep Case Wagon	D325	131	—	Vol. 2
100	8 Ton Deep Case Wagon	D326	132	—	Vol. 2
103	20 Ton Flat Wagon (6 wheeled)	D329	133	—	Vol. 2
104	20 Ton Flat Wagon	D585	134	—	Vol. 2
105	20 Ton Flat Wagon	D722	135	—	Vol. 2
106	12 Ton Flat Case Wagon	D327	137	—	Vol. 2
107	15 Ton Flat Case Wagon	D327A	138	—	Vol. 2
108	15 Ton Flat Case Wagon	D883	139	—	Vol. 2
109	12 Ton Girder Wagon	D338	141	—	Vol. 2
110	15 Ton Girder Wagon	D337	140	—	Vol. 2
111	6 Ton Glass Wagon	D323	142	—	Vol. 2
112	10 Ton Glass Wagon	D723	143	—	Vol. 2
113	60 Ton Gun Truck	D331	179	—	Vol. 2
114	100 Ton Gun Truck	D622	180	—	Vol. 2
115	6 Ton Gunpowder Van	D384	100	154	Vol. 1
116	7 Ton Gunpowder Van	D385	101	155	Vol. 1
118	16 Ton Hollow Bolster Wagons	D321	144	—	Vol. 2
119	20 Ton Hollow Bolster Wagons	D341	145	—	Vol. 2
120	30 Ton Hollow Bolster Wagons	D320	146	—	Vol. 2
121	36 Ton Hollow Bolster Wagons	D319	147	—	Vol. 2
123	25 Ton Hot Armour Plate Truck	D724	148	—	Vol. 2
124	40 Ton Hot Armour Plate Truck	D725	149	—	Vol. 2
125	12 Ton Implement Wagon	D202	150	—	Vol. 2
126	12 Ton Implement Wagon	D727	151	—	Vol. 2
127	15 Ton Implement Wagon	D313	152	—	Vol. 2
128	18 Ton Implement Wagon	D314	153	—	Vol. 2
129	18 Ton Implement Wagon	D728	154	—	Vol. 2
130	5 Ton Ventilated Van for carrying Motor Cars etc.	D833	104	160	Vol. 1
131	6 Ton Iron Skeleton Wagon	D324	155	—	Vol. 2
132	8 Ton Van for carrying Road Vehicle	D367	106	162	Vol. 1
133	5 Ton Covered Van for carrying Motor Cars	D368	102	157	Vol. 1
134	5 Ton Covered Van for carrying Motor Cars	D369	103	158	Vol. 1
135	2060 Gall. Creosote Tank Wagon	D729	117	—	Vol. 2
136	10 Ton Traction Wagon	D333	156	—	Vol. 2
137	12 Ton Traction Wagon	D730	157	—	Vol. 2
139	15 Ton Tramcar Engine Wagon	D312	158	—	Vol. 2
140	6 Ton Wheel Wagon	D315	159	—	Vol. 2
141	20 Ton Wheel Wagon	D316	160	—	Vol. 2
142	10 Ton Wood Skeleton Wagon	D317	161	—	Vol. 2
143	Weighing Machine Adjusting Van	D731	107	164	Vol. 1
144	Weighing Machine Adjusting Van	D834	108	167	Vol. 1
145	10 Ton Goods Brake Van	D390	184	—	Vol. 2
146	10 Ton Goods Brake Van (hand & vac. complete)	D391	185	—	Vol. 2
147	10 Ton Goods Brake Van & Mail Van (A. V. through pipe)	D392	195	—	Vol. 2
148	20 Ton Goods Brake Van	D393	186	—	Vol. 2
149	20 Ton Goods Brake Van (hand & vac. complete)	D394	187	—	Vol. 2
150	Crane Match Wagon	D738	199	—	Vol. 2
151	Gas Store Holder Truck	D588	123	—	Vol. 2

In 1911 there appeared in the Railway & Travel Monthly a three-part article by Fred Crocker, who was employed at Derby. This article, which described the works as at that date, also takes the reader back to the very early days of the Midland Railway Company and it was felt that this article was so interesting it should be reproduced with very little editing. Some of the original sketches used have been redrawn and these, in conjunction with other drawings and photographs and information contained in this chapter, are all that is known of the early days of Midland freight stock development.

RAILWAY CARRIAGE AND WAGON BUILDING AT DERBY
BY FRED CROCKER

First Part of Article

When a small body of Coal-Masters met at the "Sun" Inn at Eastwood on the 16th of August, 1832, to discuss the possibility of extending the Mansfield and Pinxton tramway to Derby and Leicester, to adopt steam power in the place of horse haulage, and, incidentally, to provide a more extensive outlet for the produce of their mines; the Committee of seven gentlemen, who were instructed to take "such steps as they may deem expedient" to give effect to the resolution of the meeting, little thought that the vast undertaking now known as the Midland Railway Company would be the ultimate result of their deliberations.

It was not until the year 1838 that contracts were given out for the construction of the Midland Counties Railway, and at the same time sufficient rolling stock was ordered to work the Derby and Nottingham portion of the new line, which was duly opened on the 30th of May, 1839, amidst great festivities. In the following summer the Leicester portion of the line was opened for traffic.

On the 11th of May, 1840, the North Midland Railway, from Derby to Leeds, ran its first train of thirty-four carriages drawn by two engines, and containing 500 passengers, who were duly entertained to a sumptuous repast on Derby platform.

About the same time a further undertaking, the Birmingham and Derby Railway, was built, and when these three companies amalgamated in the year 1843, they formed the nucleus of the present system. Further extensions were made in all directions; in 1860 a well-known contractor, to use his own expressive words, which have now become proverbial locally, "dammed the rivers and blasted the rocks" of the Peak district, a wonderful engineering feat, which extended the line to Buxton, and from that time to the present the line has continued to grow North, East, West, and South, has crossed the seas to Ireland, and still continues to expand.

As the most central point, Derby became an important railway depot, and works were built on the site of the present Locomotive Department for the repairs of the vehicles.

Following the custom of the times, Derby Station was situated about a mile from the town, consequently land was available for extension of the Works, and the Midland has not suffered through being cramped for room, as most of the other railways have done.

Up to the year 1873 the Locomotive and Carriage and Wagon Works were combined, the carriage bodies at this time being built in a loft over the wagon shop and let down through an opening. A tale is told that a body was once built too large to pass through this opening, and the body had to be cut in two for removal and afterwards spliced, but as this tale emanates from locomotive sources it is not generally credited.

In the year 1873 it was decided to separate the departments, and, after working under somewhat crowded conditions at the old works, in 1876 a splendid site was selected on a piece of level ground about three-quarters of a mile away, where new carriage and wagon shops were designed and built on an extensive scale. At the same time ample room was allowed for future extensions, and although provision has been made for dealing with 6,426 carriages

Plate 3

The lifting shop, Derby carriage works.
Lifting a coach from its bogies.

Photograph British Rail

(about double the 1877 stock), and 128,902, or more than four times the quantity of wagons, there is still room for further extension.

The separation of the departments has had a marked influence on the design of railway carriages, not only on the Midland system, but in this country generally, as the heads of the departments have been able to devote the whole of their energy, and that of their assistants, to the improvement of carriage and wagon stock alone. When new designs have been required the assistance of the best known carriage builders in the country have been called in, and amongst other innovations the introduction of American Pullman cars, and the abolition of the second class compartment, or, more properly, the bringing of the third class to the second class standard, and the abolition of the third, owe their inception to the broad-minded policy of Sir James Allport and the Directors of 1875.

Whilst the Board was directing a policy of improvement that appealed to the general public, Mr. Thos. G. Clayton, who had taken over the management of the depart-

ment in 1873, was introducing new features in carriage design of a more technical nature, many of which have only just been adopted as new on some railways. For instance, in 1875 bogie carriages 54 feet long and having clerestory roofs were built, and these had more roomy compartments than is allowed by many of the railways at the present time. The third class compartments were separated by full partitions, whilst seats and backs were well trimmed, in fact these vehicles were fully up to present day requirements. Previous to the opening of the new works, most of the Midland Railway carriages were built by private contractors, but when the new premises were in working order in 1877 the staff was increased to about 2,000 men and most of the stock built at home.

In 1875 trouble was experienced with privately owned wagons, some of which were so badly designed and maintained as to be a source of danger, and a resolution was adopted by the Directors to purchase a number of these at a fair valuation from the owners and to raise £1,000,000 for the purpose. This was duly carried into effect, com-

5

mencing in the year 1882, and from that time to 1895 some 66,813 wagons were bought and put into safe working order for running on the railway. A special shop was built for dealing with this work fully equipped with a smithy and wood and ironworking machinery. Since that time these vehicles have been replaced with new ones of the Midland Railway standard type.

On January 1st, 1885, a private trader's wagon left the rails at Penistone on the M. S. & L. (now Great Central) Railway through an axle breaking. A portion of the goods train fouled the opposite line and a passenger train ran into this obstruction with disastrous results. In reporting upon this accident to the Board of Trade the Government Inspector stated that no less than 141 wagon axles had broken during 1883, and he advised that railways should exercise control over the design and construction of privately owned wagons. This recommendation was considered by a committee of railway officials, and in due course a private owners' specification was drawn up and adopted by the various railways. No wagons were allowed to run without being inspected and registered by one of the railways.

The first specification issued was practically a copy of the Midland standard design, and under the direction of the Railway Clearing House this has been added to until at the present time it embraces all the types of privately owned railway wagons in general use.

In January, 1902, Mr. Clayton retired, and Mr. David Bain, who was at that time in the service of the North-Eastern Railway, was appointed his successor.

In addition to the Derby Works, there are 26 outside repairing depots, the largest of these being at Bromsgrove, which is fully equipped with machinery and accommodation, that has been used in cases of emergency, for building new wagons, and no less than 3,200 men are employed at these out-stations.

At the present time the headquarters works at Derby have a ground area of 128 acres, of which 36 are covered. There are 36 miles of railway on which three or four engines with a full staff of shunters are at work night and day bringing in and taking out materials and rolling stock; 4,000 men and 200 women are employed here, bringing the total number of employees who work under Mr. Bain's direction up to 7,400.

It takes one about three hours to have a comprehensive look round the Works, but with the aid of the plan on page 10 we hope to give the reader a personally conducted tour "on paper" in a much shorter time; we can afterwards look at a few of the old and new methods of designing and building carriages and wagons which become interesting by contrast with each other.

Passing under the bridge from the main line at "A" (see plan on page 10) vehicles can be shunted forward to the right and enter the shops by means of steam driven traversers at the North end, or they can be taken through the sorting sidings to "B", a distance of a mile, and passed into the shops the opposite way.

The first building to claim our attention is the General Offices "1," with accommodation for the Superintendent, Accountant, clerical staff and draughtsmen. The coach builder of 1840, who came to work in a top hat and followed trade traditions handed down from mediaeval times, required no drawings other than those he could make himself with a piece of chalk or with his foot on the dusty earth. The draughtsmen of the same date came after the work was finished and made a picture, matters of detail being a secondary consideration. At the present time the work follows the draughtsman; details are all important, and the making of the finished pictures left to the photographer. Leaving the offices we pass on to the Works.

The spirit of romance that inspired Longfellow's poem, "The Village Blacksmith," naturally follows when watching the processes involved in a large manufactory. The mighty hammers shaping semi-molten masses of metal, the cupola blast weaving mysterious fleeces of slag wool to hang in festoons from roof and walls, the whirling saw tearing through the heart of a century-old giant of the forest, the hydraulic presses bending, punching, and forcing the reluctant steel into familiar forms of railway usefulness, all these have interest for even the most casual observer.

Not always, however, is this interest maintained, although something is generally found to instruct, to interest, or to amuse. Once the writer conducted a party round the Derby Carriage Works, shop after shop was visited without any appearance of animation on the part of the visitors until at last the smithy was reached. Suddenly the party became excited and collected round one of the fires where a smith and his mates were working on a very ordinary piece of work. What could be the cause of the excitement? This was clear when one of the strikers on finding himself the centre of attraction threw down his hammer and fairly bolted. The poor man, who had seen service in India, had had his arms decorated by a Babu tattoo artist with designs of a decidedly Oriental character, which, on his return to western civilisation, he would have given many weeks' pay to have removed. An attempt that was made by a well-meaning friend to clothe some of the figures had made matters rather worse than better.

Bearing to the right we come to the timber gantry "2," fitted with a rope-driven travelling crane, by which the fifty-seven odd miles of oak, hickory, and pitch pine logs at

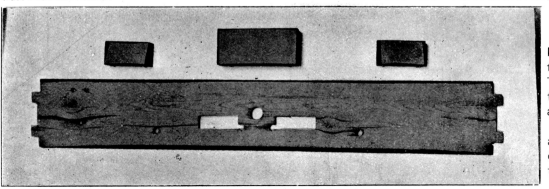

Plate 4 Shrinkage of timber in seasoning. The thick lines on the four pieces show the amount of shrinkage.

The bottom view also shows the effect of using unseasoned timber.

present in stock will be conveyed to a cross-cutting saw, and from thence into the saw-mill "3."

Here they are cut into scantlings of varying size and then taken to one of the four drying sheds "4," to undergo the process of natural seasoning, which time and experience have proved to be the only one suitable for carriage and wagon timbers. If the pieces of timber stored in these sheds were placed end to end they would extend for well over 2,000 miles. The seasoning process occupies about two years, and although there is apparently a large amount of capital lying idle, the time spent in the drying sheds, even from a shareholder's point of view, is the most profitable period of the timber's usefulness.

The illustration on page 6 from a photograph, shows the shrinkage that takes place during the process of seasoning, the black outline giving the original size to which the pieces were cut. This shows two pieces of American red oak on each side at the top and the loss is exceptional. Stettin, the centre piece, and Odessa oaks shrink much less, ¼-inch in 12 inches being the average. The lower portion of the illustration shows the effect of using unseasoned wood. This piece shrunk fully ¾-inch after being used as one of the main timbers of a coal wagon, and the vehicle had to be stopped for its replacement. Quantities of Australian Jarrah, Karri, and Blackbutt are used in addition to the hard woods mentioned previously, but the pieces are generally obtained cut roughly to size. In the shed marked "5" on the plan, mahogany panels and fancy woods for interior work, consisting principally of walnut, sycamore, and wainscot oak are stored, the stock being about 1¼ million superficial feet, or 190 miles run if the pieces are placed end to end. Fir timbers, mostly of 9 by 3 and 7 by 2½ inch red and white deal, are stocked out of doors for seasoning, and the stock exceeds 1,100 miles, in addition to which some eighty-six miles have been sawn into boards and planed ready for use.

Our illustration on page 8 of the interior of the sawmill shows the heavy circular saws and log frames at work, the moulding, shaping, mortising, and other wood finishing machines being nearer the building shops at the other end. The wing on the extreme left of the mill is used for the preparation of wagon timbers, on the right is an extension that was built in 1897, and fitted with light machines for dealing with carriage interior work. A good feature of this building is the absence of overhead shafting and pulleys, these being contained in a cellar underneath, and this has greatly simplified the change from steam to electric motor driving which is now taking place.

Some of the 140 odd machines are of the latest pattern, others are equal to them in spite of having seen over thirty years' service, two notable veterans being the planning and moulding machines, which deal with an average of over six million feet run of timber per annum.

Each piece of timber is machined to a pattern or template, the object of which is to make all parts of a vehicle interchangeable, and this standardization is so complete that a wagon repairer at far away Carlisle or Bristol can replace damaged parts of a twenty years-old vehicle, with the aid of such simple tools as a hammer and spanner.

As many of the employees live a considerable distance from the works, the time allowed for meals is insufficient for them to go to their homes, and mess-rooms have been provided by the Midland Railway (marked "6" on the plan), with seating accommodation for 2,000 men. Cooking ranges, with cook attendants for warming meals and making tea and coffee, are supplied.

Some years ago the clergy of Derby arranged for one of their number to take a short service with an address during the breakfast time on three or four days a week, and a rostrum with an organ was fitted up in one of the mess-rooms for the purpose. This has become a popular feature amongst the workmen and seats in the "preaching room" are in great demand.

The wagon building shop ("7" on the plan), has a capacity for turning out about 140 wagons per week, painted complete and ready for traffic. Two steam traversers are at work continuously bringing up ironwork, etc., from the metalworking shops and taking away the finished vehicles.

Shop No. 8 is the carriage building, or to use the correct term the "body building" shop. The under carriages are made of steel in the shop marked "16" on the plan, and are brought to No. 8 to be fitted with bodies by the body makers. There is room here for eighty medium sized vehicles to be built at one time.

Shops Nos. 9 and 10 are used for carriage repairing, and are equipped with vertical hydraulic rams for lifting the carriage bodies off the underframes and wheels. A careful record is kept of the mileage run by the heavy main line carriages and when this has reached about 70,000 miles, the vehicle is returned to Derby for the wheels, axles, and bearings to be taken out and overhauled. So carefully is the examination of these parts attended to that the failure of a carriage axle or wheel has not occurred on the Midland Railway or its joint lines during the last thirty years. The bearings also receive very careful attention and after being repaired each carriage is run on a trial train without passengers for about thirty miles, as many trips as are considered necessary; the vehicles are afterwards worked on slow trains for a few days before they are allowed to run at express speed. These precautions have secured immunity from stoppages that used frequently to occur in the old days through heated bearings.

The shop marked "11" on the plan will accommodate about 120 carriages of average size and is used for repairs, with the exception of a few bays on the right hand side in which new vehicles are placed to have the interior fittings fixed. This position is convenient for the cabinet makers and carriage finishers, who work in the adjacent shop "12," and for the French polishers who have a portion of this building partitioned off for their use. A few wood-working machines for carving, sandpapering, and light joinery work are run by steam power to minimise hard labour as much as possible.

The building marked "13" is known as the trimming shop and is used for the preparation of the upholstery and trimmings in cloth, moquette, lace, silk, velvet, and the many materials of a similar nature that add to our comfort when travelling. A small gas engine drives a cloth cutting band knife and a number of sewing machines. A large portion of this shop is partitioned off for the accommodation of some 200 women and girls who are engaged in upholstering and French polishing.

The painting and varnishing of a railway carriage is a serious matter, as the exterior of each vehicle receives from

Interior of the saw mill.

The carriage finishers' and joiners' shop.

eight to twenty coats of paint or varnish, and this accounts for the comparatively large size of the buildings Nos. 14 and 15, with an area of over 4½ acres, which are used for the class of work, and in which are more than three miles of railway track. As each coat of paint takes a day or more to dry, the full process of painting occupies about three weeks, and to see the amount of labour involved in rubbing the surface with pumice stone to a state of absolute smoothness, after some of the principal coats have been applied, reminds one how often the "game of patience" has to be played in the workshop.

Four large steam traversers are continually at work between the various carriage shops, shunting the vehicles in and out of the buildings.

No. 16 is a building that has been recently erected and fitted with the best examples of electrically-driven overhead cranes for lifting the heavier types of carriages, also with motor-driven machines for the building of steel carriage underframes and steel wagons. This shop covers a surface area of about 2¾ acres. In addition to electricity, hydraulic, compressed air and vacuum producing plants are installed, the latter being used for brake testing and carriage cleaning purposes. Formerly it was the practice to beat the cushions of the carriages with sticks to raise the dust, then to brush it off; now powerful vacuum extractors are passed over the trimmings and these suck up every particle of dust, which is conveyed by pipes to iron receptacles from which it is cleared as occasion requires.

No. 17 is the fitting, iron working machine, and wheel making shop. This building, which covers more than two acres, contains over 700 machines of different types, including a complete plant for the manufacture of teak centred wheels for carriages, gas furnaces for heating tyres

before they are shrunk on, hydraulic rams for forcing wheels on to the axles and a number of heavy lathes for turning and boring wheels. The wheel balancing machine is worth attention; on this a pair of carriage wheels revolve at a speed equal to upwards of sixty miles per hour at the rim. The journals or bearing ends of the axles are balanced on flexible springs and if the wheels are not true vibration is set up. By holding a piece of chalk to the rim, the heavier part of the diameter is marked, the machine stopped and the defect counterbalanced by attaching a weight in a position determined by experience. This process is continued until the pair of wheels revolve without any apparent vibration.

No. 18 is a new building in which is installed three electrically-driven batteries of drop forging stamps, a heavy forging machine, and other down-to-date plant, with oil fuel furnaces for heating the metal.

In No. 19 the centres of wagon wheels are made by means of hydraulic machinery. There are several presses for welding the spokes into the rims, and a larger one, capable of exerting a pressure of 1,000 tons, which forms the boss and punches a hole five inches in diameter through the centre, which is 7 inches in thickness, at one operation; the necessary furnaces for heating the metal are also provided.

The forge (No. 20 on plan) is equipped with heavy steam hammers for forging drawgear and the heavier carriage and wagon ironwork, also with hydraulic machines for bending axle guards, coupling links, and other ironwork. Adjacent to this building are 9 Wilson type gas producers, in which small coal is converted into gas for use in the steam generating boilers for the hammers, and in the furnaces for heating the metal to be forged, etc.

The smithy (No. 21 on plan), in addition to 92 smiths'

Plate 5 Locomotive employed in shunting carriages and wagons in the shops at Derby.   *Photograph British Rail*

Placing a carriage bogie on its wheels in the lifting shop.

The drop-stamping shop.

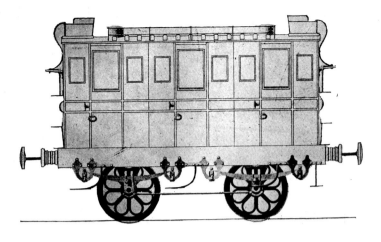

Plate 6 A working drawing provided for the use of railway carriage builders 70 years ago.

Plate 7 The wagon wheel making sh

Portion of one of a set of four working drawings such as are now provided for the use of carriage builders at Derby carriage works.

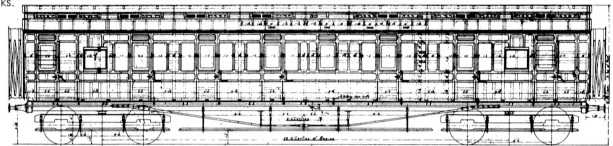

Figure 1 Layout of Derby carriage & wagon works.

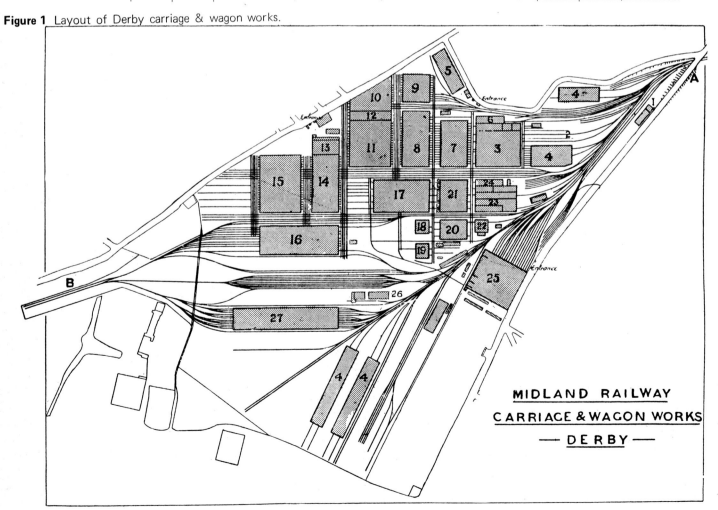

MIDLAND RAILWAY
CARRIAGE & WAGON WORKS
— DERBY —

hearths, is provided with steam hammers of various descriptions, circular saws for metal, punching and shearing presses, nut and bolt making machines and a very complete spring making plant.

In the brass foundry (No. 22 on plan) the ornamental castings used for decorating the interior of carriages are produced, in addition to heavier articles such as locks and handles, gas fittings and bearings for the various vehicles.

The iron foundry (No. 23 on plan) with its two cupolas, can turn out 130 tons of castings per week and is equipped with the best types of moulding, core making, and fettling machines that can be obtained.

No. 24 is the general stores. To give a list of the various materials that are dealt with here in a twelve-month would fill an issue of the *Railway and Travel Monthly*, and to describe the various tests, practical, mechanical, and chemical to which these are submitted by the Midland Railway's experts before they are accepted from the manufacturers would take up more space than we can afford.

In the same block of buildings are tin-workers' shops and a brass-finishing shop. The offices of the Assistant Superintendent (Mr. H. R. Haigh, whose service with the Midland Railway dates from 1875), the Works Manager's, and drawing, testing, correspondence, and time-keeping offices are also situated in this block.

The building No. 25 will accommodate about 400 railway wagons for repairs and painting, and in addition the 7,000 odd road vehicles and 8,000 odd barrows and hand-carts owned by the Midland Railway are built and repaired in this shop.

The grease factory and storing shed (No. 26), owing to the inflammable nature of the materials dealt with, is well away from the other shops. About seven tons of lubricating grease per day is manufactured to a well tested formula, which is varied to suit the different seasons of the year.

No. 27 is a shed used for storing about 200 special vehicles that are not in every day use, and, if time permits, newly painted carriages are kept here for a few days before being sent into traffic, for the varnish to harden.

We hope to deal with the design and construction of some of the ancient and modern types of Midland Railway carriages and wagons in our next issue.

Second Part of Article

It is interesting to trace the evolution of the modern railway carriage, and to note the various influences that have been at work to produce our vehicles as we now know them. As the effective life of a coach is only from twenty-five to thirty years, none of the vehicles used in the early days of railways are in existence, but the Midland Railway possess a fairly complete set of drawings, dating back some eighty years, and from these, a few of which we are able to reproduce, we can gather what our forefathers had to put up with when taking a railway journey.

The first private carriage known in this country was presented to Queen Elizabeth by a Dutchman. In 1555 Walter Rippon built a carriage for the Earl of Rutland, from which it will be seen that the coachbuilder of 1830 had some three hundred years of trade tradition to work upon when designing his railway carriage, consequently he worked on the methods to which he was accustomed, and

the result was a hybrid between a stage carriage and a tram wagon. An interesting example of this type of vehicle, a model of which is now in the possession of Mr. Bain, was used at the opening of the Stockton and Darlington Railway in 1825.

This carriage (or stage coach)? was named the "Experiment," and was hired for the occasion from a coach proprietor, of Darlington, who had a stage carriage body of the period placed on a special under-frame, mounted on tramway wheels. To give the vehicle a more symmetrical appearance, a "boot" was placed at both ends, which also enabled the carriage to be driven on the return journey without being turned round. It was drawn by one horse, and commenced running October 10th, 1825.

When the first part of the Midland Railway was opened in 1840, although some progress had been made in the art of railway carriage building, the third class coaches were open, and were without seats, but the sides were panelled, and the stage carriage idea of design was followed, by using "sweep mouldings" on the bottom panels, at the ends, and at each corner on either side of the door.

The second class carriage of the same period was provided with a roof, but the sides were open much the same as our present day cattle wagons are built.

In the first class carriage the stage coach type of design was still more apparent. The vehicle of 1839, having the appearance of three bodies placed end to end on one under-frame, this effect being produced by curved mouldings on the panels and D-shaped side windows. End steps and driving seats were fitted to all covered vehicles, providing accommodation for four or six outside passengers on each carriage, and allowing for the use of the reliable horse as a tractor in the event of the doubtful engine of the period failing. A certain portion of the vehicles were fitted with brakes, which were operated by a brakesman, who rode on the roof of the end vehicle. At first the carriages were loosely coupled, and the brake could only be applied to the particular vehicle on which the guard happened to be riding. Luggage was carried on the roofs of the carriages, iron rails being employed to keep the packages from falling off, with tarpaulins as a protection from the weather. Each large station was provided with a few planks, which were placed in a sloping position from the platform to the carriage roof, by means of which the luggage could be rolled off. No doubt accidents occurred at times, resulting in damage to the packages, but the passengers of this early period accepted this as incidental to the serious undertaking of a railway journey.

The carriages at this time were made from 14 to 16 feet long by from 4 ft. 9 in. to 6 feet wide, and 4 ft. 10½ in. high in the centre. A first class coach would weigh from 4½ to 5 tons; a second class from 4 to 4½ tons; and a third from 3 to 4 tons; in fact, the whole train (sometimes even including the engine) would weigh about the same as one modern sleeping or dining carriage.

The passenger traffic on the tramways, which ran in conjunction with the railways, was worked by means of horses, and an illustration exists which shows a first and second class composite that was used on the parent line of the Midland Railway, the Mansfield and Pinxton Tramway, in 1848, which becomes interesting by contrast when compared with the vehicles and method of traction employed

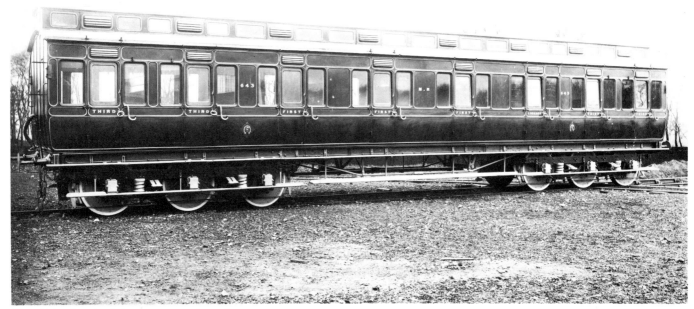

Plate 8 A six-wheel bogie composite of 1875. These coaches were 54 feet long, and had clerestory roofs.

Photograph British Rail

Plate 9 Six-wheel, four compartment composite coach with luggage locker.

Photograph British Rail

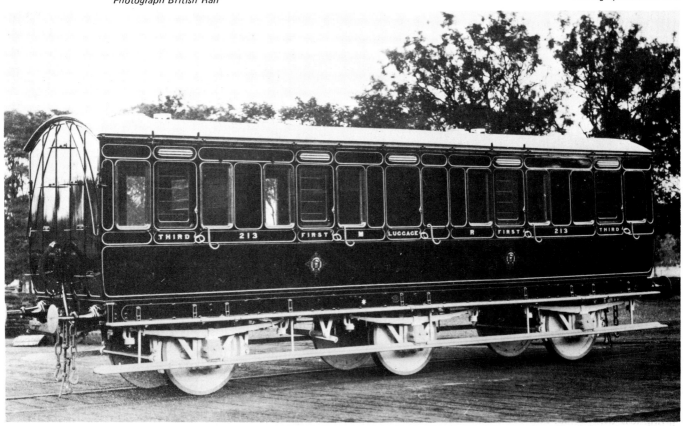

on the Heysham Tramway at the present day which are, in effect, normal carriages. It is also interesting to note that one of the chief arguments used in opposition to steam traction on railways was that the breeding of horses would fall into disuse, yet the Midland Railway employs over 5,000 of these useful animals for haulage purposes at the present day.

From 1830 to 1850 may be classed as the first period of railway carriage construction, when the types we have referred to were in general use. Whether there was trouble through the outside guards' heads damaging the bridge, or vice versa, is not recorded, but after 1850 the practice of putting seats on the carriage roofs was discontinued. The luggage continued to be carried on the outside for a further period of twenty years, and many vehicles were running well into the 'seventies with the luggage rails still on the roof.

The great exhibition of 1851 had a marked influence on railway construction, and the passengers who travelled up to London by the ordinary trains, or by one of the many excursions that were organised at the time, were so impressed with the value of the railway as an improved means of conveyance that a boom in railroad building resulted. Money was easily obtained for schemes of the wildest description, and lines with no possible prospect of paying were fully or partly made. Most of these, however, have become valuable through the discovery of minerals or from other causes, and have been absorbed into one or other of the trunk lines.

The mention of excursion trains calls our attention to the different ideas which prevail amongst Traffic Managers of the present day from those of former times. It was customary to keep worn-out, or out of date stock, for this class of traffic and the open thirds of the '"Forties," or the "knee lockers" of the '"Sixties" were retained many years after they should have been converted into firewood, to be used for the torture of excursionists. Some of the railways are still behind the times in this respect, and probably consider that the special vestibule excursion trains, with dining-cars attached, now provided by the Midland Railway are in advance of the times.

The second period of railway carriage design on the Midland Railway lasted from 1850 to 1870. The first class vehicles were at first much the same as before, except that the removal of the roof seats allowed more height inside, which permitted the use of ventilators over the doors and side windows. A print of a first-class carriage of this period is interesting in that it illustrates the coachbuilder's idea of placing one single & two double bodies on an underframe. While it has not been possible to use this picture it will be noted that the bottom corners at the rear end are turned up and finished with a scroll in imitation of the "jacks" that are used on State carriages of the time for the leather brace suspension. When a particularly fine railway carriage was built it was customary to have these "jacks" at both ends, and in some cases they were carved and the headstocks and other portions of the exterior were decorated in a similar manner, much the same as a showman's van of the present day.

The third class carriages were now provided with roofs, seats and windows, although at first great economy of space was obtained by crowding five compartments into 20 feet, giving less than 4 feet between the partitions, which were

only carried up to the height of the seat back, and from 16 to 18 inches between the unpadded "knife board" seats on which the passengers travelled with interlocked knees. Notwithstanding the economy of space, several ingenious schemes for passenger packing were patented and submitted to the Railway Companies, but as they were somewhat expensive to carry out and would not comply with certain Board of Trade regulations, the public escaped. At first, the windows were fitted in the doors only, but as one of the regulations referred to above demanded 60 inches of window area for each passenger, "pigeon-holes" were cut on each side of the door and glazed after the vehicles were built, and on one branch of the Midland Railway the cresent-shaped lights were used in third class carriages of the period.

Great improvements were made in the under-gear; screw coupling with continuous draw gear were adopted for the carriages with improved spring buffers.

Although the speed was not great, serious accidents occurred through the wheel tyres, which were secured to the rims with rivets or screws, breaking, and in 1855 the first continuous fastening was patented to obviate this danger, consisting of a dovetailed key-ring, which was further improved by the Mansell retaining ring, patented in 1862, modifications of which are now in general use.

The second class carriages of this period were similar to the third, with the exception that a little more room was allowed between the partitions and there was a little padding on the seats and backs.

The lighting of the carriages at this time left much to be desired. Although the letter of the Board of Trade regulations stipulating that not less than two lamps should be provided in each carriage was strictly adhered to, the spirit in which it was carried out was more ingenious than satisfactory. The lamps when properly trimmed were of about one candle power illumination, but this was considerably reduced after the light had been burning a short time, or when the shaking of the carriage spilled the oil to swill round the under-side of the glass globe; further, each first and second class compartment was only allowed one half of a lamp, which was placed in the top of the partition between two compartments.

The patent records of the time show many clever inventions relating to railway vehicles. One suggests a set of long pneumatic buffers between the carriages with large air cushions on the end of each vehicle, the idea being to absorb the shock in cases of collision between two trains. Another suggested building the end vehicles with an inclined plane and a set of rails running the length of the train over the roofs, so that when trains met one would simply run up the inclined plane in front, over the other, and down at the back! Something of this kind would simplify single line working!! A certain amount of skill on the part of the drivers would be required in dodging the bridges and tunnels, but a journey on a busy line would provide as much excitement as a trip in an aeroplane on a windy day. Compressed air, vacuum, the steam pressure brakes were patented before 1850, and in 1856 a modern idea was anticipated in a patent for a steam warming apparatus continuous throughout the train. A gentleman, probably of a nautical turn of mind, invented a brake in which the guard threw overboard an anchor attached to a cable which was wound round a drum in the van. The anchor was supposed to catch in the sleepers, and the guard retarded the train by braking the drum with a hand-spike. The recovery of the anchor was not arranged for, possibly the cable would be cut if the guard was in a hurry, but of course these little things are mere matters of detail.

Previous to 1870 railway carriages were mostly built by private builders, a notable firm being Wright's, of Birmingham, which eventually became the Metropolitan Railway Carriage and Wagon Co., Ltd. There were several other firms connected with this branch of industry, of which Birmingham was the most important centre, and a large export trade was carried on, vehicles being constructed and sent to all parts of the world. This led to a combination of English and American ideas of carriage design, one of the notable effects of which was the introduction of the American car truck, to which the term "bogie" (a name that was previously used here for small heavy trucks) was applied. This permitted vehicles of greatly increased length to travel safely round curves, and when what may be termed the third period of carriage design (from 1870 onwards) was reached, full advantage was taken of the idea, and the length of the vehicles increased from 25 feet to 54 feet. In the stock of this period the last survival of the stage carriage design disappeared, and the "sweep" mouldings, which in the preceding sets of designs were used only on the lower side panels at the ends, were omitted altogether.

Early in the "Seventies" the question of using continuous brakes was discussed, and experiments were conducted on a large scale with compressed air, vacuum, continuous chain and hydraulic pressure. Eventually the Midland Railway adopted the vacuum brake, but this, at first, was of a very elementary character. The method of producing the vacuum was similar to that in use at the present day, but the apparatus used on the vehicles consisted of collapsible cylinders, much like the bellows of a concertina, one end of which was attached to the frame of the carriage, the other through a system of levers to the Brake blocks.

The cylinders were connected by a continuous coupled pipe to the engine, and when air was exhausted from this pipe the cylinders collapsed like a closed concertina, thus applying the brakes. Many improvements were made, a great number of which were invented by officials of the Midland Railway, the most notable being the alteration from the simple vacuum system described above to one of an automatic character, in which the brakes apply when air is admitted to the train pipe, either by the guard or driver, or by accidental fracture of the pipe.

In 1872 a standard size of 6 feet between the partitions was adopted for third class, and 7 ft. 3 in. for first class compartments. These dimensions exceeded previous measurements by more than a foot. The 54 feet composite carriage of this period, which is illustrated on page 12, shows a marked improvement in design on previous types. In addition to being mounted on bogies, it will be noticed that this vehicle has a lantern or clerestory roof, an undoubted advantage from a hygienic point of view, but a doubtful one when we take into consideration the methods of warming in vogue at the time, or the want of them. This feature was only used on some fifty vehicles, but the general design was adopted as a standard to which all carriages were built for a period of nearly thirty years. A great number of the carriages built at this period were mounted on six wheels,

a general type being the composite, two firsts, two thirds and a luggage compartment (see illustration on the bottom of page 12), and a five compartment third, both of which were 31 feet long. In 1886, when lavatories were introduced for ordinary stock, the luggage compartment was made into two first class lavatories, and later, in 1889, the middle compartment of the third class carriage was altered to provide the same accommodation for third class passengers. When the new works at Derby were in full swing, a number of carriages ranging in length from 40 to 47 feet, mounted on four-wheeled bogies were constructed, and this class of vehicle was adopted as a standard for main line traffic.

Four first and four third class Pullman carriages were imported in 1874 to make up two experimental trains. The first class cars were 56 feet long, and the third 50 ft. 6 ins., and the vehicles were fitted with central buffers and couplings. The experiment of running these trains resulted in failure, as the public objected to the large open compartments on the ground that they were draughty; further, the seats were somewhat crowded and uncomfortable, and suffered by comparison with the Midland new type of stock of the same date. These vehicles were eventually fitted with side buffers and used for holiday and excursion traffic.

At the same time arrangements were made with the Pullman Company to provide and maintain a number of parlour and sleeping cars under a contract which eventually terminated in 1888, when the Midland Railway purchased the cars and took them into its own stock. These vehicles were exceedingly well built, the interiors being particularly fine examples of cabinet work, and this, no doubt, led to more attention being paid to inside decoration on English railway carriages and to a sub-division of work, the coach builders, who formerly did the whole of the building, confining themselves to the bodies, the interior work being carried out by cabinet-makers or carriage finishers. Third class Pullman cars were tried as an experiment, but the public did not take to them, and they were eventually used as offices and messrooms.

The possibility of building carriages of steel was taken into consideration in 1875, and two vehicles were imported from Belgium by the Midland Railway built entirely of iron and steel, but they were found so unsatisfactory from a passenger's point of view that they ran a very short time. The question of this style of construction as a preventative of fire in the event of an accident is one that is periodically discussed in the Press. Unfortunately, in the upholstery of the seats and the passengers' luggage and clothing there is enough inflammable matter to produce disastrous results, and, with metal construction, to this would be added the terror of being cut to pieces by the sharp edges of steel panels and angle bars, or to be imprisoned in a steel cage. Anyone who has seen the wreck of a covered steel wagon after an accident will appreciate this danger.

Great improvements were made in axles, steel being substituted for faggoted iron, and the wheels were forced on by hydraulic pressure instead of being keyed on. A further improvement was made by rolling the tyres of steel in a continuous ring instead of welding them. Attention was also given to the bearings, and instead of a grease-fed axle-box, oil lubricators, which acted on the under-side of the journal, were substituted and perfected, until stoppages from hot bearings became practically unknown. The lighting was improved by placing a better type of lamp in each compartment, and, later, by the use of gas, which ruined a lucrative trade in candles carried on by the book-stalls. At first the gas was carried in a large collapsible bag, but, later, a heavy gas, made from shale oil, which could be compressed into iron cylinders fixed under the carriages, was substituted. The latest development is the use of incandescent mantles, which give a very clear and satisfactory light. A number of vehicles are now fitted with electric light, the current being supplied by a dynamo driven from the axle of the carriage when the vehicle is running over a certain speed, or from twenty-four accumulators when the dynamo is cut off. It has been stated that by driving off the carriage axle the light is obtained for nothing. Actually, the power is supplied by the locomotive just as much as if the dynamos were placed on the engine and driven direct.

Some of the Pullman carriages were heated with a coke burning stove and hot water pipe, but with this exception, no attempt was made to warm the carriages in an effective manner till well on in the "Eighties." At first a system of hot water pipe supplied from the engine was employed, but this was at times a little too effective, and the term "roasting apparatus," applied by some irate passengers, was no doubt merited to some extent. Later, low pressure steam was tested with regulators in each compartment, which, with various improvements that have been made is in satisfactory use at the present time.

In 1891 Derby built its first dining carriage.

This vehicle which is 60 ft. long is still running, and is fully equipped with a gas cooking stove and all appliances for preparing meals en route, also with a very completely fitted pantry. The experiment was a success, and at the present time the Midland Railway has 115 dining carriages in regular traffic, some of the later ones of Mr. Bain's design being 65 feet long and 9 feet wide.

In 1896 new designs for carriage stock were prepared, when the cross dimensions were increased to the full extent allowed by the structure gauge, the six feet width of 1840 being augmented to 8 ft. 6 in., and 4 ft. 10½ in. head room in the centre, which satisfied our grandfathers, was raised to 8 ft. 6 in. The clerestory became a feature of all main line stock, and the third class compartments were considerably increased in width from partition to partition. The fitting of the interiors of the third class compartments with polished mahogany, and the elaboration of the first class, by the introduction of carved, and incised and gilded work, greatly increased the labour of the carriage finishers, which was further augmented in 1897 by the introduction of corridor carriages. A feature of this stock was the return to square, cornered windows, which simplified the framing, but in practice it has been found that after a time, the weather gets into the square cornered joints rendering them liable to rot. They are also more difficult to clean, and a return has been made to the round cornered windows with outside mouldings to correspond. For the same reason, in Mr. Bain's later designs, the use of carving and projecting mouldings have been discontinued, variety in decoration being obtained by the contrast of highly polished fancy woods; corners and projections for the harbouring of dust are eliminated wherever possible.

The 65-ft. sleeping carriages are fine examples of modern carriage building. They are brought out to 9 feet wide at the waist, except just at the ends, to give the greatest pos-

sible lengths to the berths, and are fitted with every luxury it is possible to conceive to relieve the tedium of the journey to Scotland. There are one double and nine single-berth compartments in each carriage, which has a smoke room at one end. The interior is finished in light wainscot oak with sycamore panels relieved with walnut mouldings, and the seats and berths are upholstered in terry moquette of an artistic design. The vehicles are warmed by means of steam pipes and heaters, and are equipped with electric light. There is also an attendant's compartment, fitted with a small gas heater for providing coffee and other light refreshments.

Third Part of Article

At the time of the opening of the first steam railway in 1825, the type of wagon used on the tramways had become practically standardized, and from what we can gather from contemporary prints, these vehicles save that on lines without edge rails, where the flange had been transferred from the rails to the wheels was much the same as the vehicles running on the Little Eaton tramway, which had been in existence for over one hundred years. No doubt the same type of wagon was used on the Mansfield and Pinxton tramway, and although we have no illustration of one of them, it will be noticed that the wagon shown in Fig. 3 had two sets of buffers, an outer pair at each end for use on the railway, and an inner set to allow for interchange traffic with the tramway wagons. Considerable progress had been made in vehicle design in the ten years preceding the opening of the Midland Railway. The wheels, which had been previously placed outside the frame, were now brought inside to run underneath the vehicle, and the simple pedestal bearing, which was good enough for a speed of four or five miles an hour on the tramways, was replaced with an axle-box, fitted with a brass bearing. The ends of the axles were extended through the boss of the wheel, to form bearing journals, which were turned. The first axle-boxes had an open recess at the top, with two holes, through which oil ran down to the brass bearing; later the recess was made larger to hold 1½ lbs. of grease, and fitted with a hinged lid. The draw-bar passed through the wagon from end to end, and was joined by means of a sleeve connection with two cotters, but had no spring. The coupling chains had hooks at the ends, some of which were fitted with locking links to prevent uncoupling when the chains were slack. The wagons were fitted with bearing springs and lever brakes with wooden blocks. The axles were made of wrought iron, with 6 in. by 3 in. journals, and the usual load was from 5 to 6 tons. Another illustration Fig. 4 shows a low-sided wagon, built in 1844, for general goods traffic, and it will be noticed that this vehicle is not provided with doors. The cattle wagons were open at the top and the goods brake vans were built with one half covered and the other open, the brake screw being fitted at the end of the open portion.

About the year 1855 spring buffers, which had previously been used on a few vehicles only, became general for wagon as well as carriage stock, and the laminated combined buffing and draw-spring, which is now used on nearly all English rolling-stock, was then introduced.

Plate 10 Derby Works in 1890. This interesting photograph shows a number of private owner mineral wagons being taken into Midland stock. Note the dumb buffers, some vehicles in private owner livery, others repainted and lettered 'MR'. Those in the foreground have carried 'MR' for some time and one should be noted for its hopper bottom, the two wagons in the centre and right, with buffers are original Midland vehicles, all others seem to be ex Private Owners.

Photograph British Rail

Plate 11 The ugliest vehicle constructed at Derby! New type of snow plough for use between Carlisle and Hellifield.

Photograph British Rail

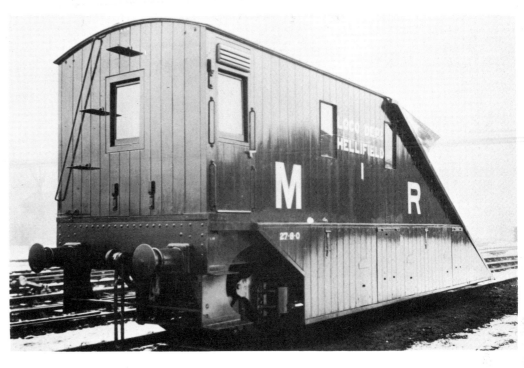

The question of the gauge, or distance between the rails, was much discussed in the 'Forties.' The use of 4 ft. 8½ in. on the tramways was practically a standard, and Stephenson, on the railways with which he was connected as engineer, adopted this dimension. On the other hand, Brunel advocated a broader gauge of 7 ft. 0¾ in., and the Great Western Railway, of which he was the engineer, with the Western connections, were made to this gauge. Some of the lines which are now part of the Midland Railway system were built to the broad gauge, which led to great difficulties when the railways found that it was to their mutual interest to work together in interchanging traffic. To meet the case, the broad gauge lines were provided with three lines of rails, in some cases at the junctions only, in others the whole length of the line, to allow of both broad and narrow gauge trains being run. Shunting operations with mixed gauge wagons were carried out by means of a heavy buffer plank, which led to many accidents, both to stock and men. Eventually, as the smaller lines became absorbed by the larger, the gauge question, as far as the Midland was concerned, resolved itself into the adoption of the narrow.

A quotation from "Our Iron Roads" by Williams, written in 1852, shows that the wagon stock of that period was unsatisfactory "by the recent introduction of patent axleboxes, this evil" (the heating of railway carriage axles) "will be to a great extent obviated in future. The same praise cannot be bestowed on the goods wagons, as in no portion of the railway system has so little improvement been made as in this. The fracture of axles is frequent, the mode of coupling defective, and the want of spring buffers, or even buffers of the same height and width, renders the destruction of property enormous."

From this we gather that the improvements introduced between 1850 and 1860 were badly needed, and in addition to a general standardizing of buffer heights, widths, and coupling lengths, greater attention was given to details, resulting in improvements in axleboxes and wheels, in the latter the stud or rivet fastening previously used for securing

the tyres was replaced with a continuous ring, which prevented pieces breaking away in the event of fracture. The axles were now made of faggoted iron, that is to say, a number of small bars of iron were tied into a bundle and welded together, which gave much greater strength than when the axle was forged, and turned out a single large iron bar. In practice we find that these axles, after many years running are liable to become "seamy" through the joints, where the bars are welded together, breaking away, and the fractures that occurred were generally traceable to this fault. The flaw commenced at the end of one of these seams and gradually worked its way across the journal until it eventually broke in two. The method of securing the wheels to the axles by means of keys was also a source of danger. A fracture often started at the end of a keyway, or the key worked loose, allowing the wheel to shift on the axle, causing a derailment. Improvements in steel manufacture by Bessemer and others enabled the axles to be made of mild steel, cheaper than of faggoted iron, and in practice it has been found that, with the precautions now taken in testing and examining these steel axles, breakages are practically unknown with ordinary wear and tear. A great improvement in tyres was effected by taking a bloom of steel, making a hole in the centre, which was enlarged until it could be placed in a special set of rolls, which formed the tyre in a continuous ring without welding. Previously the tyre bars of iron were bent into a ring and welded up, the weld being a prolific source of danger from its liability to fracture.

The danger to railway servants of having to go between the wagons for coupling purposes was recognised at an early period, and in 1861 a coupling device, the invention of a Mr. Osborne, was tested by way of experiment. Although the arrangement is comparatively simple, it seems to have quickly gone the way of many similar devices that have been invented and tested since. Automatic and mechanical railway couplings, judging by the patent records, seem to have an especial attraction for the inventor. It is a question,

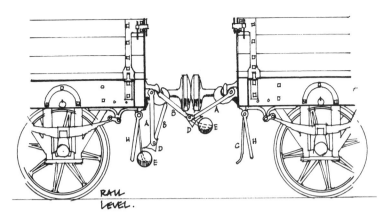

RAIL
LEVEL.

Figure 2 Osborne's wagon couplings patented c1860.
Figure 3 A goods wagon with two sets of buffers, used in 1839 on a railway now forming part of the Midland Railway.
Figure 4 Midland Railway low sided wagon built in 1844.

*All drawings by Courtesy of
A. Whitehead*

Figure 2

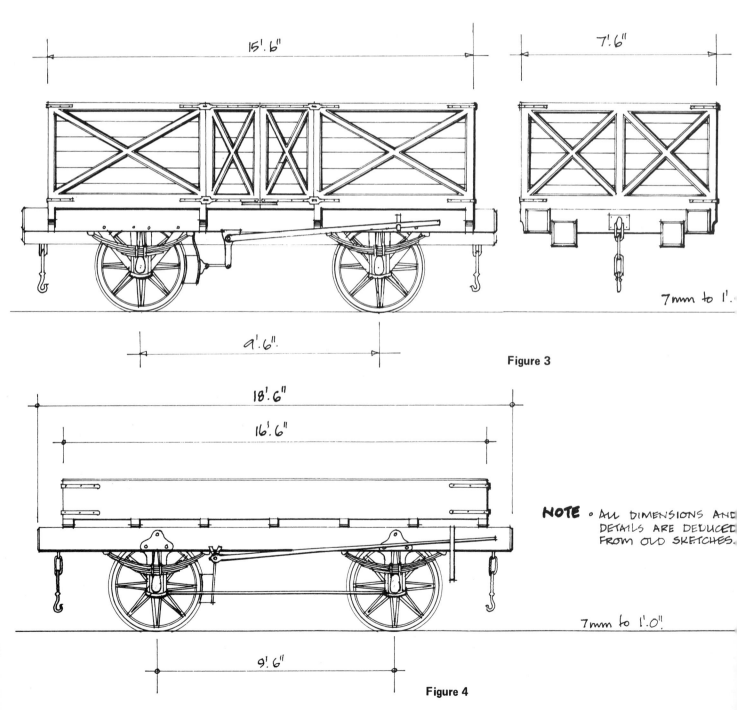

15'.6"

7'.6"

9'.6"

7mm to 1'.

Figure 3

18'.6"

16'.6"

NOTE . ALL DIMENSIONS AND DETAILS ARE DEDUCED FROM OLD SKETCHES.

7mm to 1'.0"

9'.6"

Figure 4

18

however, whether any improvement can be made that will be more suitable for the English method of marshalling trains in sorting siding, than the links and hooks in present use and the shunting pole.

Early in the "'Sixties" it was found that the traffic in minerals was much more important on the railways than was at first expected, and high and low-sided wagons suitable for this class of traffic, much the same as are in use at the present day, were designed with solid plank sides and falling doors. At first these vehicles were built to carry 6 tons (later, the load was 8 tons), and although the bulk of the 100,000 odd wagons in stock of this class are registered to carry 8 tons, the tendency at the present time is to increase the capacity up to 10 or 12 tons.

From a tour of the works at Derby it will be noticed that the actual building of one of these wagons has been reduced to the utmost limits of simplicity. The woodwork is planed up by machinery marked out from iron patterns; every joint is prepared and every hole bored by high speed machines. The ironwork is forged or stamped to exact patterns, and all holes are drilled to make similar parts absolutely interchangeable with each other. Consequently, when the wagon-maker takes a job in hand, the parts are prepared and laid out and by 9 a.m. a start is made to build the wagon by three men. By 12 o'clock the same day the wagon has made considerable progress towards completion, and at 4 o'clock the wagon-makers have finished and handed the wagon over to the lifters who place the wheels underneath, and, as far as running is concerned, the wagon is ready for traffic; but, of course, the familiar lead-colour paint with the large "M.R." have to be put on, and although each coat takes a very short time to apply, it takes a day to dry, consequently four or five days elapse before the vehicle is actually ready for the trial trips and eventually for the road. All Midland Railway new wagons are now fitted with practically the same bearings as are used on carriages, and, instead of grease, oil is used for lubricating purposes. This will enable the trains to be run at a much higher speed, and allow for an increase of express goods trains when occasion demands; also, it effects a saving of at least 15 per cent. in the tractive force required to draw the train.

Some thirty years ago there was an outcry amongst railway engineers that the supply of timber would soon become exhausted, and on some of the lines expensive plants were laid down for the manufacture of steel wagons. The Midland Railway adopted a policy of—to use a current political term—"wait and see." A few steel wagons were built by way of experiment, but it was found that the carriage of coal was particularly destructive to the steel work, which rusted away in a comparatively short time, and that a wooden wagon had a longer life by several years than one of steel; further, the cost of repairs, and the facility with which they could be carried out, especially at outstations, was greatly in favour of the wooden vehicle. The anticipated timber famine has not yet come, and a comparison of the maintenance cost per vehicle of the railways, as given in the half-yearly reports show that the Midland Railway adopted what was, at least, an economical policy.

As the bulk of the traffic on English railways consists of loads that seldom reach more than 6 or 8 tons for any particular trader, the wagons we have dealt with constitute the greater portion of the stock, but vehicles are now required for classes of traffic that were certainly not anticipated by the early railway builders. Take frozen meat for an example. This is carried in special refrigerator vans, which have the walls insulated by a triple casing of boards with the space between filled with insulating felt. The doors are hermetically sealed by means of a bar with a binding screw and handle. Nearly covering each end is a large flat iron tank which is filled from the roof with a freezing mixture of ice

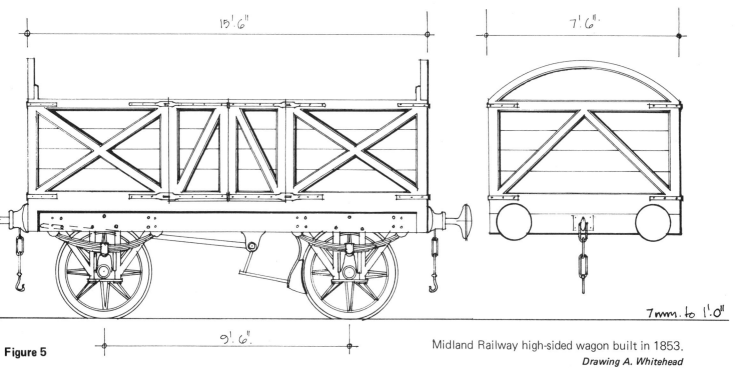

Figure 5

Midland Railway high-sided wagon built in 1853.
Drawing A. Whitehead

and salt. The vans are fitted with screw couplings, and the vacuum brake to enable the trains to run at express speed.

A still more delicate passenger on the railway than frozen meat, is the banana. This fruit requires especial "coddling," and the vans are built for its conveyance with ventilators that may be opened or closed as the season requires, they are also fitted with the steam warming apparatus to keep up the temperature in case of frost. These vans are marked in large letters "B X S." The "B" denotes that the vehicle is used for banana traffic, "X" that it is fitted with bearings and brake to run at express speed, and "S" that it is equipped with steam warming apparatus.

Although the bulk of the Midland Railway's wagons are built of wood, the company possess a number of high capacity vehicles made of steel or iron, including a quantity ot 30-ton bogie coal wagons, which are employed when a regular point to point traffic can be assured in sufficient quantities to warrant their use. The company also conveys armour plates in large quantities from the Sheffield district to the various shipbuilding yards on 40-ton bogie trucks built especially for this class of work. In addition to these

are some 40 different types of special wagons, with loading capacities of from 6 to 50 tons, which are used for the conveyance of various articles such as boilers, glass, ships' anchors, masts, large wheels and pulleys, guns weighing from 60 to 80 tons, parts of machines or structures of a bulky or peculiar shape, some of which tax the ingenuity of the loaders to the utmost and make them devoutly wish Brunel had been before Stephenson and given them the broad gauge.

Some of these articles require special fittings to enable them to be carried at all, and in some cases they are loaded to overhang the 6-feet way to such an extent as to foul the opposite line, necessitating the blocking of one set of rails and working as a single line.

The snow plough is not generally required on English railways, but the Midland Railway finds these vehicles, one of which we illustrate, very useful for clearing away the winter drifts, which accumulate in an amazingly short time on the Westmorland fells. These vehicles have the distinction of being the least ornamental of any that are turned out of Derby Works.

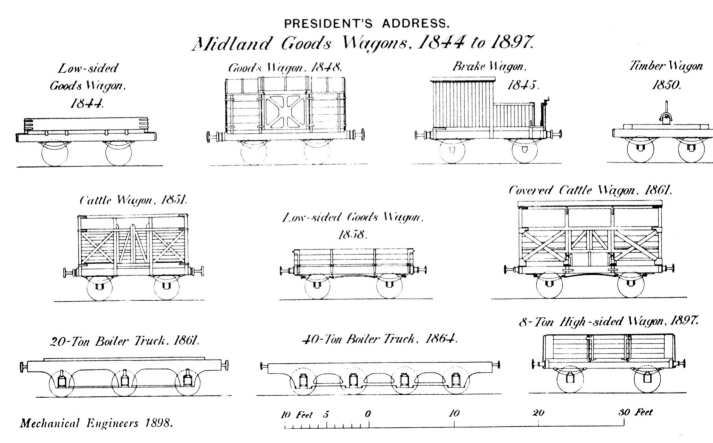

PRESITENT'S ADDRESS.
Midland Goods Wagons, 1844 to 1897.

Low-sided Goods Wagon. 1844.

Goods Wagon. 1848.

Brake Wagon, 1845.

Timber Wagon 1850.

Cattle Wagon. 1851.

Low-sided Goods Wagon. 1858.

Covered Cattle Wagon. 1861.

20-Ton Boiler Truck. 1861.

40-Ton Boiler Truck. 1864.

8-Ton High-sided Wagon. 1897.

Mechanical Engineers 1898.

10 Feet 5   0   10   20   30 Feet

Figure 6 Diagram of Midland wagons used during S.W. Johnson's address to the Institution of Mechanical Engineers in 1898. The Goods Wagon of 1844 is the subject of Figure 4. The Cattle Wagon of 1851 is featured in Figure 19. The Low Goods of 1858 or its descendant is illus-trated in Plate 2 but, regrettably, no pictures are known to exist of the 'Covered Goods Van' of 1848, the Brake Wagon of 1845, or the 1864 Boiler Truck. The others are dealt with in the relevant chapters.

As previously noted, very little has been recorded about very early wagon construction and it is believed that this extract, with drawings from the Proceedings of the Inst. Mech. Engineers will be of interest. It is a paper read by Mr. William A. Adams of Birmingham in 1852 and while it does not deal entirely with Midland stock it does refer to vehicles of a type in service with the Midland Railway and for this reason was considered worthy of inclusion. Some editing has taken place if only to ensure a continuity of Fig. nos. but the old spellings have been retained.

ON IMPROVEMENT IN THE CONSTRUCTION AND MATERIALS OF
RAILWAY WAGGONS

The improvements described in the present Paper consist principally in the substitution of wrought iron for wood in the construction of the under-frame of railway waggons.

In the commencement of 1851, the attention of the writer was directed to the construction of a large number of waggons for the conveyance of coal, which were to be hired for a term of years, and in which, consequently, the desideratum to be aimed at was, the construction of such wagons as should commercially be the least costly in maintenance, and at the same time the most lasting in ultimate duration, with due regard to first cost.

Experience had shown, that without large and costly repairs and replacements, the life of an ordinary wood under-frame does not exceed a much longer period than ten years; whilst at the same time the experience of the Great Western Railway had proved that iron under-frames, when properly constructed, continue after many years' work in excellent condition.

In a former paper (see Proceedings, January, 1851), the writer brought before the Institution the question of the substitution of wrought iron of various sections in the place of wood, in the construction of the rolling stock of railways, with the view to economise weight. A careful consideration of the subject, with the practical and scientific aid of Mr. W. P. Marshall and Mr. E. A. Cowper, has enabled the writer to produce waggons with iron under-frames and stanchions, of a simple construction, and at the same time at only a trifling excess in cost, as compared with the usual wood-framed waggons.

These waggons have been in daily work for twelve months, and about 500 of this construction are now working on the Taff Vale Railway, the Monmouthshire Railway, and the London and North Western and Midland Railways, and so far as experience shows at present, they are more economical in maintenance than the usual wood-framed waggons, and give promise of a longer life. The experience of these waggons has suggested improvements in some of the minor details of construction, but none in the main points.

The waggons to be described in the present Paper is of a somewhat different class, as the waggons first constructed were adapted for discharging coals at a shipping port by tailboard doors, and the present waggon discharges the coal at the side; but the construction of the under-frame is essentially the same.

The tare or dead weight of this waggon, to carry 6 tons, with ordinary wheels and axles, is 2 tons 19 cwt.; and the tare of waggons of precisely the same class, constructed by the writer with the same wheels and springs, is 3 tons 6 cwt.; the iron-framed waggon being 11 per cent. lighter. It is to be observed, that at the present time there is no possible commercial inducement to the private waggon-owner to reduce the dead weight, but every inducement to reduce the first cost, with due regard to maintenance and durability; and, consequently, no attention has been given to the reduction of the weight in the details of construction, whenever such reduction of weight entails any additional trouble or cost.

The construction of the improved waggon is shown in Figs 7—13.

Fig. 7, is a side elevation of the waggon;

Fig. 8, an end elevation;

Fig. 9, a transverse section of the waggon;

Fig. 10, a plan of the under frame;

Fig. 11, a longitudinal section of the end of the waggon;

Fig. 12, a section of the centre cross bearer;

Fig. 13, shows enlarged sections of the frame-iron A, the crossbearer C, and the stanchions H, specimens of which are exhibited; the smaller section of frame-iron D is used for a smaller class of waggon.

The soles AA, and head-stocks BB, are constructed of the larger frame-iron, which is 8 inches deep, 4½ inches wide on the bottom flange, and $^{13}/_{32}$ -inch thick; the weight is 20lbs. per foot. The section of the frame-iron is designed according to the principle discussed in the former Paper, so as to obtain, with the least weight of material, the greatest amount of strength under the particular circumstances to which it is subjected; the mass of metal in the section is situated at the three extreme points, vertically and horizontally, to afford the greatest strength, and the ends are thickened to $^{11}/_{16}$ -inch at the top, and $^{13}/_{16}$ -inch at the bottom. This frame-iron is rolled in a similar manner to ordinary angle iron. The corners of the frame are mitred, being sawn cold by a machine set at an angle of 45°, which ensures truth in the joint. On the under side the corners are secured by a plate 5 inches wide by $^3/_8$-inch thick, fixed with three ¾-inch rivets at each end. The top of the frame-iron is secured by a knee 2¼ x $^5/_8$-inch, fixed with three $^5/_8$ -inch rivets on the side, and two at the end. Below this

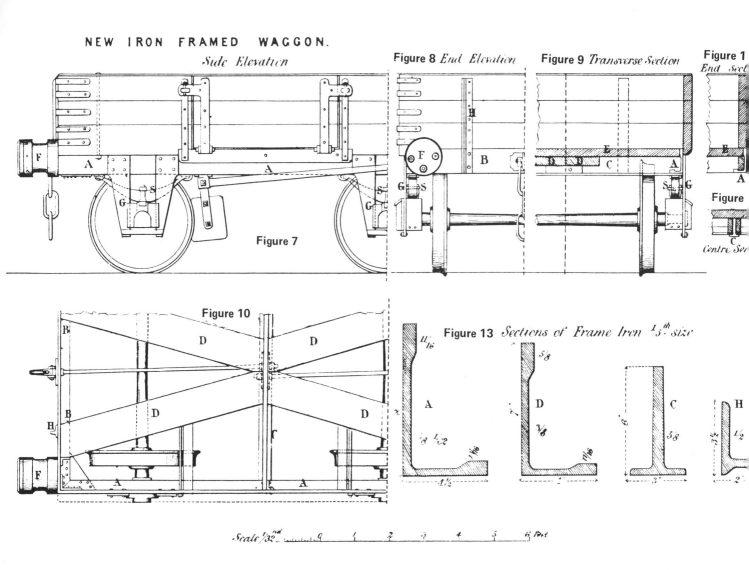

NEW IRON FRAMED WAGGON.

Side Elevation

Figure 7

Figure 8 *End Elevation*

Figure 9 *Transverse Section*

Figure 1 *End Sect*

Figure

Centre Sec

Figure 10

Figure 13 *Sections of Frame Iron 1/5th size*

Scale 1/32nd   0   1   2   3   4   5   6 Feet

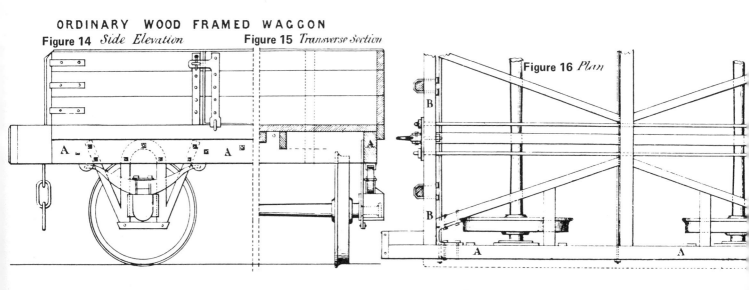

ORDINARY WOOD FRAMED WAGGON

Figure 14 *Side Elevation*

Figure 15 *Transverse Section*

Figure 16 *Plan*

the corner is further secured by an angle iron knee 3½ x ½ inch, fixed to the side with two ⅝-inch rivets, and to the end with one rivet, the other hole taking one of the bolts of the buffer-block. A little draw is given to all the rivet-holes, by which means the two pieces of frame are forced together at the corner, making a secure and rigid joint.

The cross bearer C in the centre is made of T iron, 6 x 3 inches, and ⅝ inch thick; it is notched at the ends, to fit over the bottom flange of the frame-iron, to which it is secured by two ½-inch rivets through the bottom, and an angle iron knee at the side. The cross bearer and head stocks, where weakened in the centre by boring for the draw-bar, are flitched on each side by two 5 x ⅜ inch plates.

The diagonals DD are of fir, 11 x 3 inches, laid flatways; their outer ends abut against a piece of 2-inch angle iron, rivetted to the head stocks, and they rest upon the lower flanges of the frame-iron and of the cross bearer in the centre, being packed with fir packing to bring the upper side of the diagonals flush with the under side of the floor.

The floor E is of fir, 7 x 2½ inches, laid longitudinally, and it is fitted tight inside the frame, flush with the top of the frame iron, abutting against the thickened top edge of the frame, so as to form a very strong and rigid bracing to the frame. The floor rests upon fir packings at the ends and centre, and is spiked down to the four diagonals. It is to be observed that one important advantage in this method of flooring is, that the floor forms an entire panel, bracing the under-frame in all directions, and materially assisting the end resistance of the frame at the buffer-blocks.

The buffer-blocks FF are of elm, and fixed by three ¾-inch bolts, with heads inside, and nuts recessed in the face of the buffer-block, for the convenience of tightening up when they loosen in work.

The axle-guards GG are two pieces of plate, ⅝ inch thick, and fixed with four ¾-inch rivets through each leg. The fixing of these guards being made with short rivets, measuring but one inch length between the heads, effects a perfectly firm job, and none of them have been found to loosen in work, with the exception of one or two cases, where the rivet-heads have broken off, from imperfect workmanship or material.

The waggon is mounted on the improved springs, SS, that were brought before the Institution by the writer in a former paper (see Proceedings, January and April, 1850),

which reduce the total weight 148 lbs. in the set of four springs, and the expense proportionally, with the same extent of elastic action as the ordinary springs. The spring shoes are of cast iron, fixed with a ⅝-inch bolt to the bottom flange of the frame-iron, and prevented from turning round by a lip at the back, fitting against the frame.

The stanchions, HH, to support the ends are made of tramway iron, 3½ x 2 inches, and are fixed to the frame by two ¾-inch rivets. A small cross bearer of hard wood is fixed between the frame and the diagonal, to carry the side knee.

The construction of an Ordinary Wood-framed Waggon, of the same size and class, is shown in Figs. 14, 15 and 16. Fig. 14 is a side elevation, Fig. 15 a cross section, Fig. 16 a plan. The soles, AA, and head stocks, BB, are of oak, 12 x 4½ inches, mortised together and secured by transverse bolts through the entire frame. The floor is laid crossways upon the soles: with the same height of buffers, this waggon carries the load 6½ inches higher than the iron-framed waggon.

The objects aimed at in the construction of the iron framed railway waggon described above, are—

First, increase of durability, and consequent economy in the expense of maintenance, by the substitution of iron for wood in those parts that are subjected to constant strains and concussions, tending to rack the joints and make them work loose. In wood framing this action exposes it to great injury, from wet penetrating the joints; and the wood is liable to be shaken and split; but in the iron framing the joints are fitted, iron and iron, with very short bolts and rivets, and are as rigid and durable as boiler-work; and the iron, when protected from oxidation by paint or tar, is of great durability, remaining nearly as sound as at first, after such a number of years' work as is the ordinary limit of the work to be got out of a wood frame.

The second object is diminution of weight in the frame, and consequent economy in the dead weight to be conveyed and the expense of locomotive power. This reduction of weight amounts to 11 per cent., and the resulting economy is an important consideration, as a proportionate increase of load can be conveyed at the same expense of locomotive power; but at the same time it must be marked that this point has, from commercial reasons, received but little or no attention at present, and the weight of construction is capable of much further reduction.

MIDLAND RAILWAY NUMBERING POLICY

The Company's numbering policy seems to have been to ensure that there were no gaps in the number list. Therefore, if wagon No. 500 was scrapped, a new No. 500 was built to take its place. Thus No. 500 could be a much newer vehicle than 501. So, although at first one would get a run of numbers held by a batch of wagons all built at the same time, accident or ordinary wear-and-tear could mean that individual wagons in the series might be replaced by new ones before their fellows. Alternatively, individual wagons might last years longer than the rest of their class. Another cause

of mixing up of vehicles is that traffic requirements change so that, for example, old open wagons surplus to requirements might be replaced by banana vans.

New construction often took blocks of numbers higher than those previously used, whereas, replacements and renewals often took the number of the vehicle replaced.

Examination of known running numbers given within the following chapters, will reveal some numbering trends which may have been used.

Plate 12

Although not of Midland Railway origin, these two pictures of Swansea Vale Railway wagons No. 165, **Plate No. 12** and 118, **Plate No. 13** have been included to illustrate contemporary wagon building from the 1860's. They were probably taken over by the M.R. in 1874.

Photographs—Gloucester C & W Co. Ltd

Plate 13

LOTS AND DIAGRAMS—An Explanation

Within this work the terms 'lots' and 'diagrams' etc. appear, and all the known diagrams of Midland stock are illustrated, together with details of the lot numbers and drawing numbers. It is felt that an explanation of these terms would be appropriate and, fortunately, an opportunity to include details of 'a wagon in the making' occurred.

Fig. 17 and 18 are worthy of careful study.

Fig. 17 is a copy of a minute dealing with a new design for low goods wagons and in it will be seen the word "plan". This in fact is a diagram numbered D818. On the diagram will be seen the signature approving the construction of this new design and, in due course, to general arrangement drawing 4340, authorised by lot 905 dated 6th August, 1915. Authority was given to the works to construct 100 vehicles, which almost certainly entered traffic the following year. Readers should compare Fig. 18 showing the 'Proposed'

design with the diagram issued for internal use and illustrated on page 60. The D818 is constant but the tare weight, interior depth and cubic capacities have changed. Diagrams, therefore, were used by various departments to illustrate overall dimensions and capacities. Lots were the authorisation to construct quantities of vehicles, but exterior details could alter and, because the principal dimensions remained constant, the diagram remained in use. For this reason, it is unwise to construct a model from a diagram alone, and one should use photographs in conjunction with the diagram, if general arrangement drawings are not available.

Readers will note that, wherever possible, drawing numbers are given. It is felt that, if this information was available and at some time it became possible to obtain copies of these drawings, then this information would be of considerable value to modellers.

MIDLAND RAILWAY.

Extract from the Minutes of the Traffic Committee of the Midland Railway
Company, at their Meeting held at Derby, July 22nd, 1915.

37,127 Lowsided Goods Wagons.

Figure 17

Referring to Minute No.36,442, the General
Manager recommended that in renewing the present stock of 8-tons
lowsided goods wagons, the carrying capacity be raised to 10 tons,
and that they be built to new standard dimensions shewn on the
plan submitted, the extra cost being estimated at £5 per wagon.
He explained that in addition to the advantage of the greater
loading capacity, the work of construction will be facilitated
inasmuch as the same standard underframe, wheels, drawgear,etc,
will be used as is now adopted for the 10-ton highsided wagon.

The recommendation was approved, and the matter referred
to the Carriage & Wagon Committee.

W.GUY GRANET

(Sgd) A.T.

D.Bain,Esq.,

30/7/15.

Figure 18

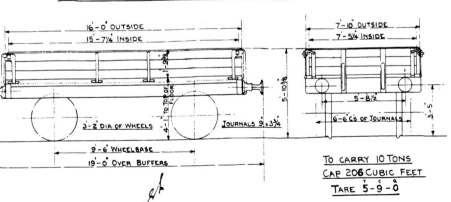

— PROPOSED —
— 10 TON LOWSIDE GOODS WAGON. —
— WITH DOORS EACH SIDE RUNNING FULL LENGTH. —

TO CARRY 10 TONS
CAP 206 CUBIC FEET
TARE 5-9-0

MIDLAND RAILWAY.
CARRIAGE & WAGON DEPARTMENT
DERBY.

D.818.

MIDLAND RAILWAY.
PHOTOGRAPHS OF WAGON STOCK.

INDEX.

Before proceeding to describe by picture and caption early Midland Railway stock built before the opening of the new works and the introduction of lot numbers, attention is drawn to **Plate No. 14**. The date and origin of the original document is unknown to the author, this copy came from the late W. O. Steel. It has proved invaluable in piecing together information and will be referred to in subsequent photograph captions. An opportunity has been taken to include some of these illustrations and they will be found in this and subsequent chapters. However, in keeping with the vagaries of the system, referred to in other chapters, some pre 1877 built stock appears in the class chapters which generally are only concerned with vehicles built from lot 1 onwards.

Photograph Author's Collection

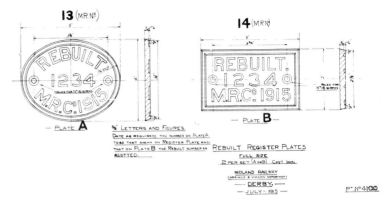

This copy of an official 1915 MR drawing describes the type of plate to be used on stock rebuilt to the current specification.

Drawing British Rail

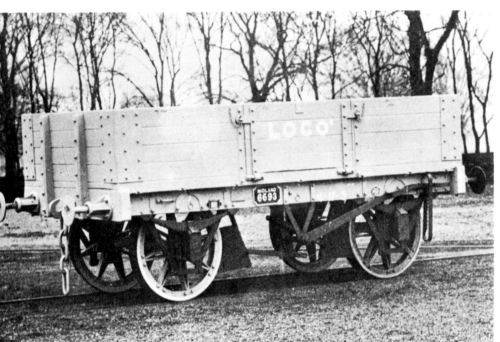

Plate 15 Loco coal wagon No. 6693, one of the 250 built in 1877 ref. no. 5 in the photographic list (see Plate No. 14.)

Attention is drawn to a number of interesting features, five link couplings, wooden brake blocks, single side brake with a single vee hanger and 8A grease axleboxes. Reference will be made again to single vee hangers but, of course, a strap support was always used to support the rod and was fixed to the inside of the solebar.

Note, also, the spoke wheel construction and the fixing bolts on the rim. The wheels appear to be in photographic grey, perhaps to highlight this feature.

Photograph British Rail

Plate 16 illustrates wagon No. 29670 which is almost certainly item No. 3 in the list of Midland wagon photographs. One hundred ballast wagons were constructed in 1875, 12' 0" over headstocks, rated to carry eight tons. Note dumb buffers, three link couplings, one side wooden brakes, solid spoke wheels and, in particular, the 'early appearance' of the blocks on the solebar against which the sides, with the protective metal plates, fell. Without doubt, these wagons would have run until early in the 20th century, maybe even until grouping; but whether they were later given spring buffers, your author cannot say—probably not. The livery is departmental stock grey, a fact discussed in Chapter 2.

Photograph British Rail

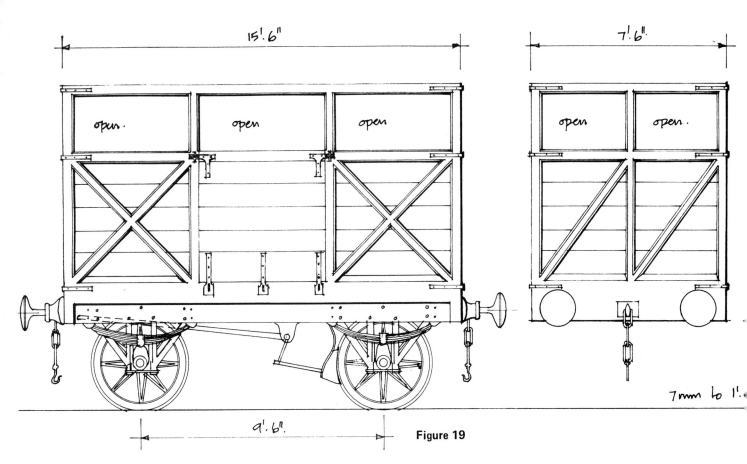

15'.6"   7'.6"

open.   open   open   open   open.

9'.6".

7mm to 1'.

Figure 19

Early Midland cattle wagons were without roofs and the drawing, Fig. 19 was made from an early print of a goods yard scene c1865. No measurements are available and the details below floor level are not distinct. It appears to be about 15' 6'' long and the drawing can only be taken as a guide to general dimensions. Particular attention is drawn to the method of side and end bracing and the side bracing is similar to the 1853 open goods construction.

Drawing A. Whitehead

NOTE:
All dimensions and details are deduced from old photographs, especially in the case of the wagon doors and underframe.
Underframe copied from high sided wagon of 1853, see Fig. 5.

Plate 17 is an illustration of a Gloucester Wagon Co. Ltd. built cattle wagon c1865 and the livery remarks in Plates 32 and 33, page 36 referring to open wagons, apply. The wagon is of the 'Medium' type. Further examples of Gloucester C & W Co. Ltd. built cattle wagons appear in Volume II.

*Photograph
George Dow Collection*

Plate 17

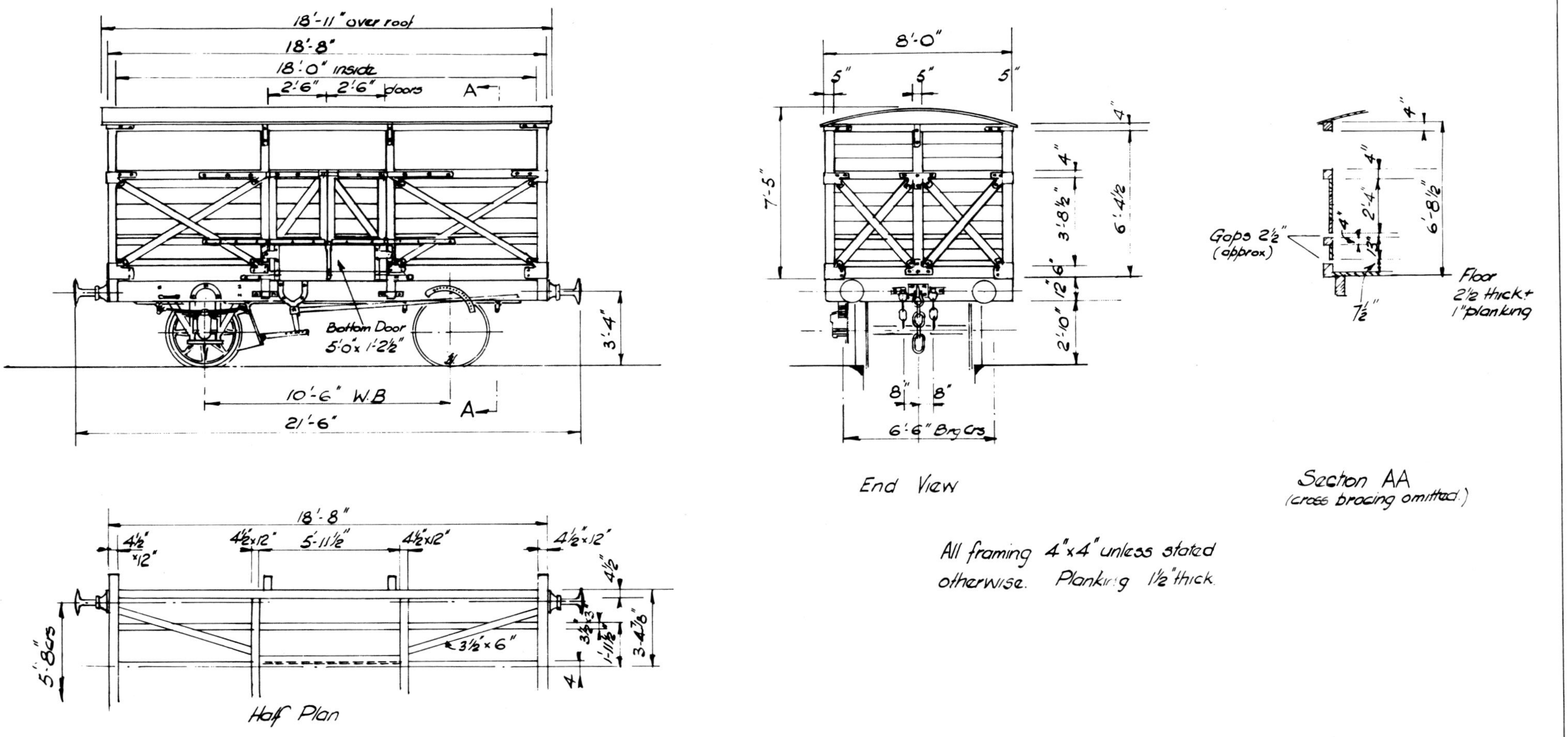
18'-11" over roof
18'-8"
18'-0" inside
2'-6" 2'-6" doors
A
Bottom Door
5'-0" x 1'-2½"
3'-4"
10'-6" W.B
21'-6"
8'-0"
5"
5"
5"
7'-5"
4"
4"
3'-8½"
6'-4½
12"
6"
2'-10"
8"
8"
6'-6" Brg Crs
End View
4"
4"
2'-4"
6'-8½"
Gaps 2½" (approx)
7½"
Floor
2½ thick + 1" planking
Section AA
(cross bracing omitted)
18'-8"
4½" x12"
4½x12"
5'-11½"
4½x12"
4½"x12"
4½"
3½
1'-11⅛"
3'-4⅞"
3½" x 6"
5'-8 crs
4
Half Plan
All framing 4"x4" unless stated otherwise. Planking 1½" thick.

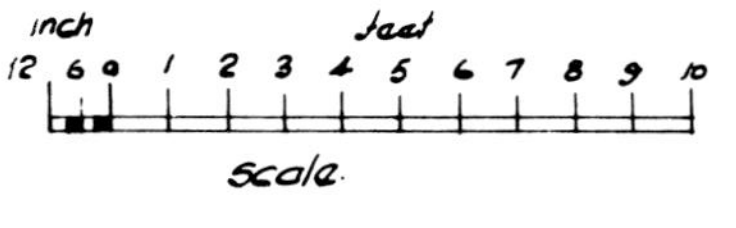
inch
feet
12 6 0 1 2 3 4 5 6 7 8 9 10
scale.

The earliest known example of a long cattle wagon is illustrated in Fig. No. 20 which shows an 18' 0" long inside vehicle as built by the Metropolitan Railway Carriage and Wagon Company in the mid-1860's. Almost certainly, these wagons would have been extinct by the turn of the century.

Drawn by G.N.I. Ibbott

Midland Railway
Covered Cattle Waggon built by Metropolitan R.C & W Ltd.
Dwn Dec 77 G.N.I.I. scale ¼" to 1 foot.

Figure 20

Plate 18

Plate 19

In 1882, the Midland commenced to purchase private owner wagons and, by 1895, some 66,000 had been acquired and many quickly withdrawn. **Plates No. 18–20**, photographed November 1893, clearly show both sides and one end of one of these wagons. Just why the photographs were taken is not known. However, attention is drawn to the condition of the livery, with the "M.R.", clearly visible on one side and almost indistinct on the other. Finally, note in **Plate 20** the swivel link coupling.

All photographs Gloucester C & W Co. Ltd.

Plate 20

Plate 21 is an illustration of a dumb buffer four plank side door wagon, with rounded ends, to which extra rails have been fitted. It is presumed this was one of the old private owner wagons, purchased by the Midland after 1882; but whether the original owner or the Midland railway company fitted the extra rails, is not known. The date of the photograph is 1894. The location was Wellingborough.

Photograph British Rail

Plate 22 was also at Wellingborough in 1894 and is presumed to be another example of an ex private owner wagon, following its purchase by the Midland Railway. The slightly higher rounded ends were typical of some private owner wagons from the period. Note the Lowther and Cameron vehicle in the background.

Photograph British Rail

Plate 21

Plate 22

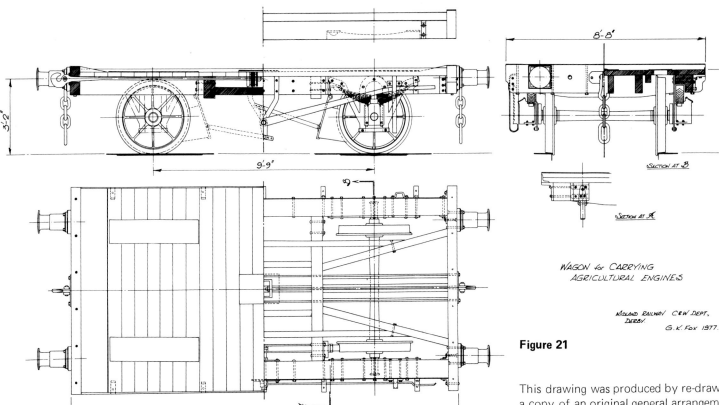

WAGON for CARRYING
AGRICULTURAL ENGINES

MIDLAND RAILWAY C&W DEPT.,
DERBY.
G.K.FOX 1977.

Figure 21

This drawing was produced by re-drawin
a copy of an original general arrangemen
drawing and depicts what, in later terms
would be a traction truck. Although th
drawing did not specify, it is believed th
was for the 20 vehicles built in 1875 an
illustrated in Plate No. 23.

Drawing G. K. Fo

Plate 23 This illustrates 8 ton implement wagon No. 27488
built in 1875. Note the early 5 link couplings, wooden brake
blocks and single side brake lever.

Photograph British Rail

Plate 23

Plate 24 Wagon No. 30554 is a 15 ton implement truck, one of twenty built in 1879 to lot No. 20, authorised on the 24.9.78—reference No. 49 in the photographic list. Drawing No. 378 referred to the construction of the batch, legend on solebar at right hand end reads "Load not to exceed 15 tons." These vehicles had all been withdrawn or renewed before the list of special vehicles dated 1915 appeared, see Fig. 126 in Volume II, and consequently no diagrams ever existed.

Photograph British Rail

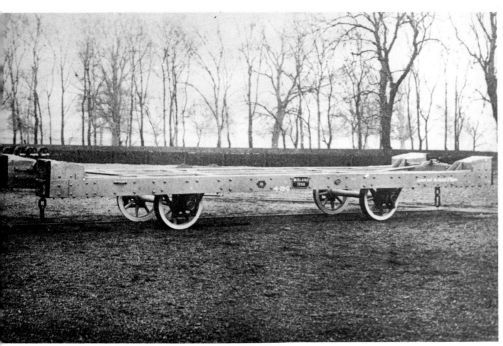

Plate 25 illustrates wagon No. 1292, an omnibus truck, built to drawing No. 388, authorized by lot 26, dated 23.12.78 This wagon appears to have no brakes whatsoever and the coupling drawbar can clearly be seen at the right hand end of the vehicle. The load was 6 tons, and the reference is No. 51 in the album of Midland wagon photographs. Note the different type of axlebox used compared with other contemporary vehicles illustrated in this chapter. Legend reads 'Load not to exceed 6 tons'.

Photograph British Rail

Plate 26. On the 15th March 1890, Lot No. 242 was authorised. Drawing No. 818 referred to the construction of a well bottom carriage truck, which became No. 390. in the carriage truck list. What the author finds so unusual about this vehicle, is the fact that it was finished in passenger livery, for use in passenger trains and, consequently, never appeared in the special wagon list. This print has been included to underline the point that the distinction between special freight stock and vehicles which could so easily have been special freight stock was indeed a very narrow one.

Photograph British Rail

33

Plate 27

Plate 28

Plate 29

Plates 27–29. These interesting illustrations show a Midland shunters truck. Very little is known about them and very few photographs are known to the author. Running Nos. included 6286, 25333 and 8455, and it appears that the basis of the vehicle is a low goods wagon (diagram 305).

Plate 27 illustrates an unidentified wagon in Midland days, while **Plates No. 28** and **No. 29** are views of wagon No. 6286. The livery of the Midland view suggests a dark body colour, either black or slate grey. The LMS vehicle has a faint LMS on the tool box and does not appear to have been painted for some time. Reference to certain other photographs of the same type of vehicle must raise doubts about livery colour, but it seems doubtful if they were painted in the freight wagon grey.

All photographs Author's Collection

Plate 30

Plate 31

Figure 5, page 19, is a drawing of an 1853 open goods wagon and **Plate No. 30** is of a similar type of vehicle—the principal difference is the door design. Fig. 5 shows a form of outside framing, while Plate 30 is flush. Since the date of Plate No. 30 is c1870, it is possible that the early design was altered, or Plate No. 30 could be a later development.

Photograph British Rail

Plate 31 shows an accident, date c 1875, location unknown. The picture has been included to illustrate a high-sided wagon with cross braced sides and a very stoutly braced end.

Photograph Author's Collection

Plates 32 and 33 illustrate two early drop side wagons. The unnumbered vehicle was built c1865 for the Spalding & Bourne Railway by Gloucester C. & W. Co. Ltd. The original print, from which this copy was made, had the words "Midland Railway" written across, and this has come out on the copy print. The black ironwork can be clearly seen. Refer also to **Plates 17, 34, 168** on pages 28, 36 and 115. Attention is again drawn to this method of painting and, whilst it is not so clear on Plate No. 33 (wagon 2141) that the ironwork is black, the original print seems to suggest this is so. Compare the Midland number plate on 2141 with wagon 13724 (**Plate 34**) and notice the different style further discussed in Chapter 2 page 5. Whilst on the subject of livery, attention is drawn to the black strapping on the other wagons behind wagon No. 2141 and, whilst one cannot be certain they are Midland vehicles, there is little doubt this is so. Note the high goods to the left; this wagon, clearly, has black ironwork.

Finally, note the tare weight on 2141 (written on the solebar) was 4-0-1.

Both plates British Rail

Plate 34 illustrates a Midland open goods wagon No. 13724 of a type which pre dates D299, see page 70. This vehicle was built by the Gloucester Carriage & Wagon Company (c1867–70) and the plate on the solebar appears to read 'To carry 8 tons'. The livery is interesting as it is a light grey body with black ironwork—a style which appears in official Gloucester C. & W. Co. photographs, and suggests this was standard Midland Railway practice. At first, it was felt this could be a photographic livery, and the matter is further discussed in Chapter. Another photograph of one of these wagons, No. 14077, taken from the 'non brake' side, clearly shows a metal capping strip on the top of the body sides and ends together with internal upright strapping bolted behind the vertical strapping (on the outside next to the door opening.) The photograph of No. 14077 shows a wagon in service, and the livery appears to have been identical to 13724.

Photograph Gloucester C. & W. Co. Ltd

Plate 35. This vehicle was in the background behind a Midland van which was
the subject of an official photograph
dated April 1896, and shows a three plank
dropside wagon, which has not been built
to a known diagram or drawing. The end
appears to have a single piece of strapping
and could be a drop end. The author's
impression is that this wagon is longer
than the normal low goods wagon.
Furthermore, the bodyside seems to be
dark in colour, probably black or red
oxide. The headstock and solebar appear
to be grey. The letter 'N' is at the left
hand end, but the legend on the right hand
end cannot be read. Note the tarpaulin
cover over axleboxes. Background views
in other photographs also reveal dirt
wagons, so more than one other example
existed.

Photograph British Rail

COVERED GOODS WAGON DEVELOPMENT

Very little is known about the development of covered goods wagons by the Midland
Railway, prior to lot 48 of 1880, but these pictures may throw some light on developments.

Plate 36 shows a vehicle in a
Midland goods yard, scene
photographed c1870. It
appears to be a covered goods
wagon with plain side and
diagonal strapping; while,
inside the van, there may
possibly be internal bracing
frames. The doors are set
away from the sides, which
suggests that they slide, but,
whether to the left or right, is
not apparent. There is no
evidence that the vehicle is
Midland but it is more likely
to be owned by that
Company than any other
Railway.

Photograph British Rail

Plate 37 illustrates a van whose door frame design is similar to the tariff van, illustrated on page 142, Plate 203. There appears to be a half opening on the roof—reference to the only other known form of van door roof is made on page 125. As far as livery is concerned, there are no visible marks of ownership, neither (on the original prints) is it possible to make out the Midland number plates. One point worth mentioning is that, on Plate 37, the ironwork is darker than the body, which could suggest the "Black Ironwork" livery, discussed in Chapter 2.

Photograph British Rail

Plate 38 shows a Swansea Vale wagon as built by Gloucester C. & W. Co. Ltd. and later taken over by the Midland Railway Company in 1874.

Photograph Gloucester C. & W. Co. Ltd.

Plate 39 illustrates a dumb buffered Midland covered wagon at the original Leicester & Swanington Railway Station at West Bridge, Leicester. Note the end and side bracing and compare with the open wagon in the accident picture, Plate No. 31. Almost certainly, these covered goods wagons were developed from the contemporary open goods vehicles.

Photograph George Dow Collection

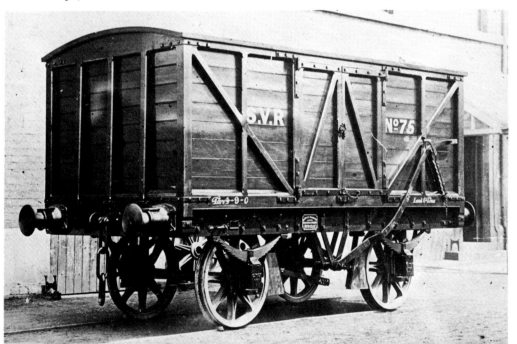

Figure 22 deals with Minute 3037 of 14th March 1895 and shows the distribution of the various vehicles which made up the stock of 112,604 traffic and 1,465 service wagons as at 31st December, 1894.

Description	Carrying capacity, tons													Total quantity
	4	5	6	8	9	10	12	15	18	20	30	40	50	
Meat vans	90													90
Passenger trains														
Fruit vans	6													6
Wagons for large packing cases		9												9
Ballast wagons			313											313
Match wagons			26	152										178
Omnibus trucks			4	1										5
Implement wagons			1	25		64		20						110
Tramcar trucks			6											6
Glass wagons			2											2
Pulley wagons			1											1
Gunpowder wagons			3	6										9
Coal wagons (as purchased)			1,572	19,688										21,260
Timber trucks			1	2,005										2,007
Coke wagons				1,351										1,351
Sleeper wagons				246	20									266
Cattle wagons				1,465										1,465
Refrigerator vans				101										101
Fruit vans				30										30
Covered goods wagons				1,746										1,746
Twin boiler trucks				6		2		4						12
Hopper bottom wagons				1,350										1,350
End door wagons				2,000										2,000
Manure wagons				20										20
Goods wagons (low side)			276	20,223										20,499
Goods wagons (high side)			1	59,435										59,436
Rail wagons							251							251
Girder wagons							12							12
Case wagons							20							20
Boiler trucks								4	7	21	1	1		34
Tramcar engine trucks								2						2
Armourplate trucks												12	1	13
Totals	96	9	2,206	109,851	20	66	283	30	7	21	1	13	1	112,604

NOTE: goods, tariff and ballast brake vans are not recorded.

D299 wagons on display, date and reason for the photograph is unknown to the author.

Photograph British Rail

Plate 4

Plates 40—41 and Figures 23—25 deal with some of the various axleboxes used by the Midland Railway. Regrettably they do not include the very earliest designs, nor was it possible to obtain photographs, in close up, to illustrate each variation used.

Plate No. 40 R.E. Lacy
Plate No. 41 A.G. Ellis

Plate 4

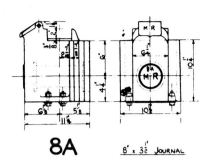

8A   8' x 3½' JOURNAL

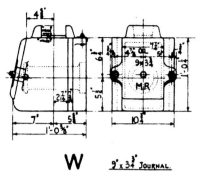

W   9' x 3¾' JOURNAL.

SUPERSEDED BY W6 & W12.

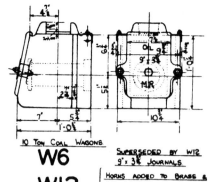

10 TON COAL WAGONS

W6
W12

SUPERSEDED BY W12
9' x 3¾' JOURNALS

HORNS ADDED TO BRASS &
BOX ALTERED TO SUIT.
TO SUPERSEDE W & W6.

8 TON WAGONS (GREASE.)

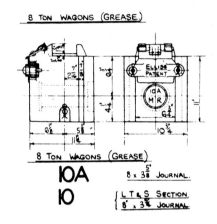

8 TON WAGONS (GREASE)

10A   8 x 3⅝' JOURNAL.

10   L.T.& S. SECTION.
           8' x 3¾' JOURNAL

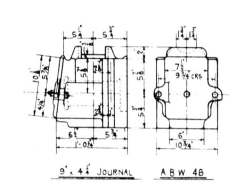

9' x 4¼' JOURNAL   A B W 48

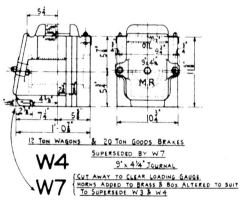

12 TON WAGONS & 20 TON GOODS BRAKES
SUPERSEDED BY W7
9' x 4¼' JOURNAL

W4

W7   CUT AWAY TO CLEAR LOADING GAUGE
           HORNS ADDED TO BRASS & BOX ALTERED TO SUIT
           TO SUPERSEDE W3 & W4

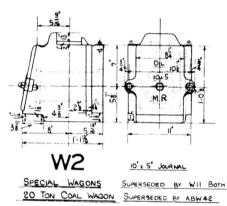

W2

SPECIAL WAGONS   SUPERSEDED BY W11 BOTH
20 TON COAL WAGON   SUPERSEDED BY ABW42

10' x 5' JOURNAL

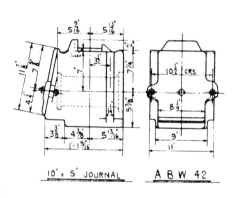

10" x 5' JOURNAL   A B W 42

W 3, W4 & W7 SUPERSEDED BY ABW 48

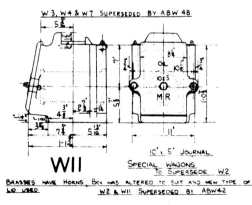

W11

10' x 5' JOURNAL

SPECIAL WAGONS
TO SUPERSEDE W2

BRASSES HAVE HORNS, BOX HAS ALTERED TO SUIT AND NEW TYPE OF
LO USED   W2 & W11 SUPERSEDED BY ABW42

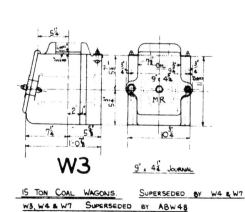

W3   9' x 4¼' JOURNAL

15 TON COAL WAGONS.   SUPERSEDED BY W4 & W7
W3, W4 & W7 SUPERSEDED BY ABW48

Figure 23

41

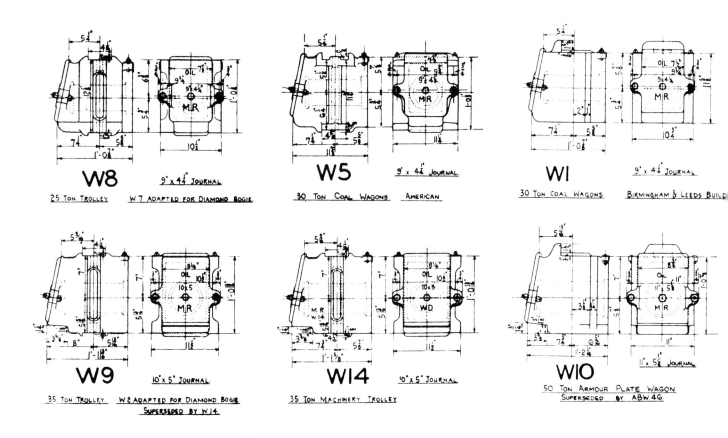

Figure 24

"Ellis 10A Grease Axlebox".

Photograph British Rail

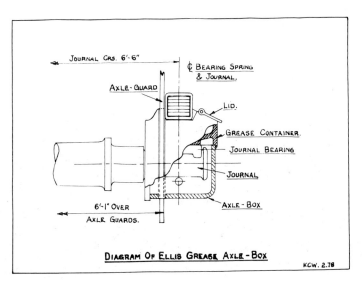

Figure 25

Ellis Axle Box

This drawing is an exploded view of a grease axle box and is typical of the type used by the Midland Railway Company. Reference in the text is made to 8A and 10A axleboxes and the 10A will be seen to be a wider version of the earlier narrow 8A box.

Drawing K.C. Woodhead

Plate 42

Experimental Brakes

During the early years of this century, the Midland tried several different forms of wagon brakes and, although little is known about the various styles, space precludes illustrations of all the variations employed; nevertheless, it is felt that Plate 41A showing the Roberts Improved Brake, together with wagons with the Spencer Brake, Plate 42 and the Haigh Brake. Plate 43 may be considered typical. Chalked upon the wagon fitted with the Roberts Improved Brake is the legend ''6 wagons fitted May 1903, Taken off Jan. 1909''.

All photographs British Rail

Plate 43

43

Plate 4[5]

The Midland sent a number of vehicles overseas and the majority were returned (*see table below*). However, there is no evidence that the 750, 20 ton covered goods were ever returned so it is presumed that these were built for the War Dept and unlike the wagon illustrated in **Plate 46** were not considered Midland Railway stock.

	No. Sent.	Returned to U.K. by 31/3/1921.
Locos.	78	78
Wagons	6,128	6,008
Coaches	6	5

Including

Lot 903—100 Meat Vans and
Lot 918—750 20-ton Covered Goods Wagons

Plate 46

Plate 45 illustrates one of the covere[d] goods wagons, and these, presumably[,] remained in Europe at the end of the War[.]

Plate 46 is included to illustrate a con[-] version from diagram 302. The autho[r] does not know how many were s[o] adapted. The date on the solebar is 9/1[7] and the picture is interesting in that the wagon is still carrying its original Midlan[d] number plates 23333.

Plate 47 illustrates a meat van of lot 90[3] as originally constructed, while **Plate 48** shows the same class of vehicle in L.M.S[.] service. This style was later used by the L.M.S. for their standard banana vans.
All photographs British Rail

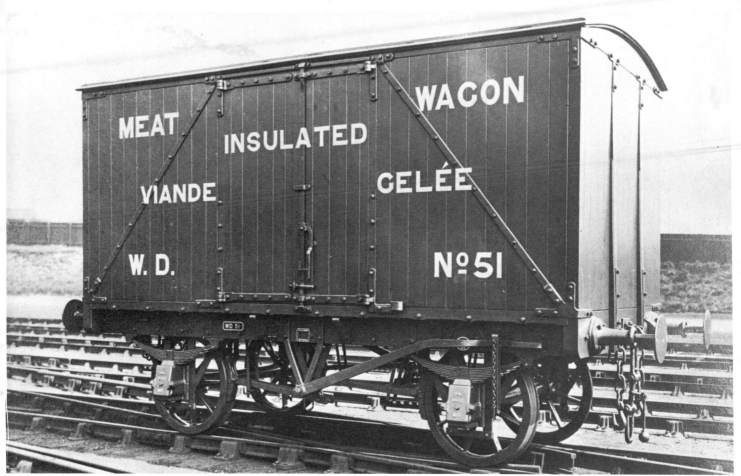

Plate 47

Plate 48

MIDLAND TRAFFIC

Plate 49 is Wellingborough 1894 and shows two ex-private owner wagons in Midland Railway ownership, plus other dumb buffered private owner wagons, together with standard Midland Railway stock.

Photograph British Rail

These Plates have been included to illustrate some typical Midland Railway traffic scenes.

Plate 50 is the Derby St. Mary's Tranship Shed on 29 March, 1911. Note the variety of barrels, bales, crates and boxes in transit. The use of straw-packed crates was widespread at this time.

Photograph British Rail

Plate 51 is Leicester on 14 October, 1912 with crates, boxes and barrels in profusion.

Photograph British Rail

Plates 52 and 53 (on next page) are of Lawley Street, Birmingham in the early years of this century. They will repay careful study by modellers to obtain the correct loads, and freight, in transit.

Photographs British Rail

Plate 53

Plate 54

Plate 54 Timber traffic, single and bogie bolsters. The nearest single bolster is interesting. It is an old dumb buffered wagon as altered with spring buffers (see also **Plate 171**, page 119).

Photograph British Rail

Plate 55 The official records suggest that ▶ this photograph was taken on the 18th August 1907 at Fletchers Foundry, Derby. The load was described as "sugar machinery". The leading vehicle is an armour plate truck built to D328 and the next three are built to D310.

Photograph British Rail

Plate 56 is another interesting train form-▶ ation at Chinley in December 1906. Starting with the goods brake van, this is the only confirmed picture of a 15 ton six-wheel vehicle. The heavy casting is on bogie wagon No. 10018 of D308 and the long tubes are on three single bolsters, but the load is only chained to the leading and trailing truck with a traction truck as the "runner". Further traction trucks are in use as runners nearer to the locomotive.

Photograph British Rail

Plate 55

Plate 56

Plate 57 at Toton 9th December, 1906, is a short train comprising a D333 traction truck as a runner plus two armour plate wagons, D328 to carry one heavy gun for the Royal Navy.

Photograph British Rail

Plate 58. Photographed at Chesterfield on the 11th June, 1910 is interesting in that the fabrication on trolley No. 10018 is followed by a goods brake van No. M2042 which precedes a heavy casting which appears to be carried between two armour plate trucks. It is presumed that the location of the goods brake between the special loads was to enable a guard to watch the load during transit. The rest of the train appears to consist of mineral traffic.

Photograph British Rail

Chapter 2   Livery-An Outline of Practice

In 'Midland Style' published by the H.M.R.S. it was recorded that most Midland wagons were painted light lead colour with the ironwork below the solebars painted black. The author of this work, George Dow, records that the earliest known specification dated July 1888 officially described the constituents of the light grey colour as 112 lb white lead (Tub or dry) 9 lb linseed oil, 9 lb turps, 30 lb dryers, 4 lb black and 36 lb boiled oil. When dry white lead was used, the linseed oil and the turps were each increased by 2½ lb. This mixture produced a light grey finish, referred to as light lead but this 'ex works' livery became darker as the vehicles progressed further in time from their last painting. **Plates 59 and 60** clearly demonstrate that Midland wagons ran in shades of grey that went from a very light colour (as originally painted) to nearly black.

In 'The L.M.S. Wagon' published by David & Charles, the question of Midland and L.M.S. grey is discussed and it now appears certain that, until 1929, when a new paint specification for freight stock was issued, Midland methods were retained and, probably, with the exceptions to be noted, the 1888 specification is a true record of how vehicles were finished.

After World War I, the Midland purchased a considerable quantity of grey paint, originally intended for warships. This was mixed with black paint and other residual paints to make a sombre dark grey which was called 'smudge'. This paint was to be used only for repainting repaired wagons and not to be used for new construction. On many pictures within these volumes, it will be noted that the initials "M.R." stand out very clearly on most wagons and this was due to the fact that the Midland used a self cleaning Oxalic paint for this purpose. Certainly, the effects can be clearly seen on **Plate No. 59**.

Apart from the goods stock which was light lead grey, ballast brake vans and ballast wagons were painted in red oxide and it is believed that petroleum and creosote tank wagons were finished in dark lead grey. Fortunately, the publisher has been able to include enough photographs to illustrate all aspects of livery and, in general, M.R. livery details are dealt with within the chapters covering specific wagon types; however, some general observations are not out of place within this chapter.

Very little is known about the early period pre-1880,

Plate 59 is a close-up from **Plate 60** to illustrate the two goods brake vans body colours contrasting the light and dark grey.

Plate 60 has been used simply to demonstrate that there is no such colour as 'Midland Grey'. Both the goods brake vans are Midland 10-ton vehicles, with other Midland vehicles around them. Whilst the colour variations are not so marked with the open wagons and partly hidden covered goods wagons, there is no doubt that it slowly went darker and darker until it was almost solid black due to the action of sulphur fumes in the atmosphere. Photographed at Wigston c1905.

Both photographs British Rail

51

however, some details have emerged, following a study of official records, as below.

Midland Order No. 2 (25/10/1853) reads: "High-sided wagons: From this date all M.R. high sided wagons with spring buffers and marked with a red cross on each side must be withdrawn from the coke traffic and used exclusively for goods, until further notice."

A further note dated 17/12/1853 emphasises that "No high-sided wagons with spring buffers must be used for goods which have not a large red cross painted on each side of them."

Midland Order No. 13 (29/4/1854) "Ballast Wagons: In future, ballast wagons which are painted red, are not to be used for the purpose of carrying any goods or mineral traffic; nor must the goods wagons be used for the conveyance or distribution of permanent way materials, except in carrying, when required, new materials from the manufacturers."

Official photographs of early Midland rolling stock are unknown, apart from those used in Chapter 1 and here it will be seen that some of these pictures illustrate the use of black painted ironwork. While it is possible that the vehicles selected for official photography were specially finished, further photographs of vehicles in traffic suggest that, at one time, some Midland wagons were so finished. However, it is not certain if this practice covered all Midland stock nor is it known for certain when it commenced or when the practice ceased. The author's view, admittedly, without confirmation, is that, prior to c1885, Midland goods stock carried black ironwork but, regrettably, the author is unable to confirm when this practice commenced.

Prior to c1880, the only mark of ownership was the cast numberplate and these, over the years, were changed in design. The earliest known style had sans serif letters forming "Midland"—smaller than the serif numerals which displayed the vehicle number (see **Plate 15**, page 27). About 1875 they were altered as **Plate 61** with 1¾" letters and 2⅛" numerals—both in the sans serif style. A variation to this for brake vans was introduced c1890 and is illustrated in **Plate 62**. As can be seen, it carried the words "Midland Brake" in two lines of 1¾" letters with the number in 2¼" numerals interposed centrally between them. The overall size of both plates was 1 ft. 1¾" x 7⅜". In 1913, a third design was introduced, **Plate 63** and this outline remained in use until 1923, when it was adopted by the L.M.S. with those letters replacing "Midland" and with the tonnage located between the bolt holes. This final style had 1½" letters and 2" numerals with an overall size of 11¼" wide x 6½" high and the colours white and black remained as before. A few Midland vehicles carried the tonnage on the plates but this was only adopted prior to the end of the Midland's separate existence.

The standard builders plate is illustrated in **Plate 64**. This together with the numberplates, was made of cast iron and painted white and black. It was 5" wide and 3⅞" high overall with the characters MRYCO and year being ¹⁷/₃₂" in height and the other letters ¹⁵/₃₂". An exactly similar plate with the word "Bromsgrove" replacing "Derby" was produced for wagons built at these works. This plate was usually located at the right hand end of the solebar.

Towards the other end of the solebar was the ticket plate, **Fig. 27**. This was made of cast iron with white letters

Plate 61 Second design of Midland wagon numberplate introduced c1875.

Photograph George Dow Collection

Plate 62 The brake van variation of the second design of Midland numberplate introduced c1890. The brake van numberplate was not changed in 1913 and this style was retained until the end of the Company's existence. Examples of this style of plate will be found in Chapter 11 and was used until 1923.

Photograph Author's Collection

Plate 63 The third design of Midland wagon numberplate introduced in 1913.

Photograph George Dow Collection

Plate 64

and edging on a black background.

The tare weight was frequently, but not always, painted in white directly onto the solebar but the study of pictures in later chapters will reveal variations.

From about 1917, rolling stock code plates began to be fitted, commencing with special vehicles and the list of codes is given in Appendix 1 Volume II, together with a drawing of a plate in **Fig. 28**. These plates were 8¼" wide, 2⅞" high with 2¼" letters. The painting style was black, with the letters and edge picked out in white.

In Feb. 1917, it was decided to paint the numbers of the goods and mineral wagons on the bodies at the right hand end of the bottom plank but, within a month, this instruction was altered to the left hand end. It was laid down that the work was to be carried out as the wagons went through the shops, but a fair number had not been dealt with by the end of the Midland's separate existence.

Apart from the fact that the grey varied in shade, examination of various pictures seems to indicate a number of styles of painting were adopted in terms of what could have been black was painted grey but, in general, the principle to be followed was:

All bodywork, including headstock and solebars, was grey. All ironwork below solebar was black. In addition, black was used for numberplates and workplates, buffer heads and couplings.

Plate 64 The Midland wagon builders plate used on all freight rolling stock.

Photograph George Dow Collection

Plate 65 The picture of wagon No. 37729 to D299 (see Chapter 3) has been included within this section to illustrate the earliest known picture of a repainted M.R. wagon in L.M.S. livery. This photograph was taken on the 27th March 1923 at Hayfield.

Photograph Sam Cowan

Van roofs seem to have varied in colour but, in service, a muddy dark grey seems reasonable.

In the November 1961 issue of Model Railway News, K. Werrett recorded that the Midland Railway painted the brake pipe standards on fully fitted stock, black, and that, on 'through pipe stock' red was the colour used, but, regrettably, the exact shade of red was not recorded. No official records regarding this policy have ever been found but the principle of using different colours to aid shunters when coupling up wagons, makes good sense and was practised on the L.N.E.R. It would, however, seem that a vermilion shade of red was most likely to have been employed.

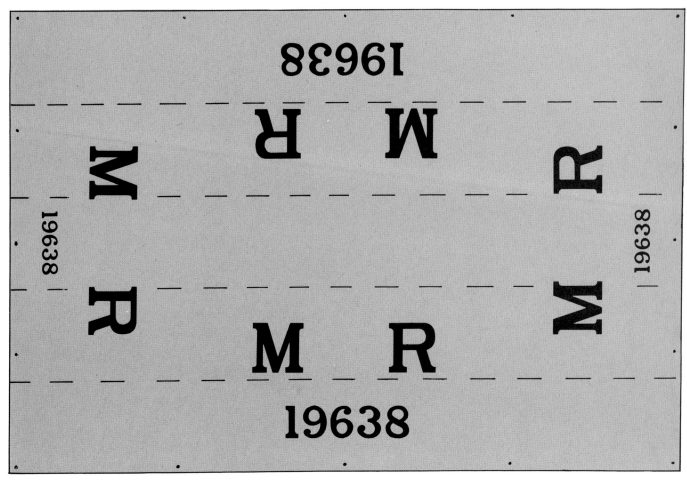

Figure 26

It is believed these sheets were 21′ 0″ x 14′ 4″ approximately.

This drawing represents the final style of Midland Railway tarpaulin sheet but the exact size is an estimate and is based upon what was being produced by the L.M.S. in the early days of the Company's existence. Midland sheets were made at 'Sheet Stores' between Derby and Nottingham and so it is reasonable to assume that the final Midland style became the L.M.S. standard. Date of manufacture not shown on drawing; it was not visible on the photograph used to produce this drawing and so the size and position could not be estimated.

Drawing P.G. Chatham

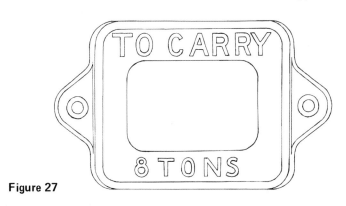

Figure 27

Figure 28

Figure 27 Midland Railway Ticket Plate
'From Midland Style' by George Dow

Figure 28 Midland Railway Code Plate
'From Midland Style' by George Dow

Plate 66 is an example of early Midland Railway tarpaulins. Unfortunately, it is not possible to see if the words 'Midland Railway' or letters 'M.R.' appear. In the author's view, the later style used by many railway companies of large lettering to indicate Company ownership, was not the practice at the time this photograph was taken.

Photograph A. G. Ellis

Plate 67 illustrates a later Midland Railway tarpaulin sheet. The numbers are about 12" high on the side and, on the original print, it is possible to see that the numbers repeated on the end are about 6" high. The legend 'M.R.' is on the sides and ends of the sheet and while it is not possible to give an exact figure, it appears to be approx. 18" high.

Photograph Author's Collection

The drawing in **Fig. 29** illustrates the various legends used by the Midland on its rolling stock, and the dates of their introduction are summarised below:—

Open goods wagons began to be lettered from the mid-1880's and were followed by goods and tariff brake vans: all used 21" initials.

Smaller letters were used on covered goods wagons and cattle wagons which began to carry the Company's initials from the early 1890's. Cattle wagons had originally carried 13 ft 3", 15 ft 6" or 17 ft 9" in white at the top left hand corner to denote small, medium and large wagons but with the introduction of the initials "M.R." the words small, medium and large began to appear. During the early years of this century, the use of "M.R." spread to almost all the vehicles within the Midlands fleet and, within the following chapters, livery information which is available, is noted. Where there is an absence of information, this is simply due to the fact that insufficient pictures exist to accurately date livery styles or changes and, in general, readers are directed towards the various chapters for specific livery information.

The information contained in **Fig. 29** and produced by P. G. Chatham, was obtained from the study of a number of photographs and attention is drawn to the following points:—

Numbers:— 6" Used on Goods Brake Vans

5" Used on Freight Stock for running numbers

4" Used when 5" not applied, e.g. Motor Car Vans

3" Used for Tare Weights

M.R:— Note that the style varies and these were drawn after studying a number of prints reproduced within these volumes, as below, plus others not illustrated:

	Plate No.
Tariff Van No. M554	392
Banana Van No. 117367	202
Meat Van No. 35464	219
Refrigerator Meat Van No. 2422	214
Motor Car Van No. 26548	227
Yeast Van No. 23029	240
Meat Van No. 114128	212
Goods Brake Van No. M965	394
Covered Fruit Van No. 30069	175
Sleeper Wagon No. 4867	166
Signal Dept. No. 167	400
Loco Coal No. 1032	125
Engineers' Dept. Van	241
Girder Wagon No. 2984	287
Loco Coal Wagon No. 56679	130
Gunpowder Van No. 32510	223
Creosote Tank Wagon No. 48	259
Oil Gas Tank Wagon No. 41642	265
Petrol Tank Wagon No. 117657	262
Engineers' Wagon No. 10077	84
Large Cattle Wagon No. 17890	252
Calf Van No. 17884	245
Medium Cattle Wagon No. 8192	248
Ballast Brake No. M121	382

A Selection of Midland Railway Goods Vehicle Insignia.

Colour: white. Black shading and backgrounds indicated in halftone. Scale: ½ inch to 1 foot.

MR

1 2 3 4 5 6 7 8 9 0

1 2 3 4 5 6 7 8 9 0

1 2 3 4 5 6 7 8 9 0

1 2 3 4 5 6 7 8 9 0

MR MR MR MR M.R MR

LOCO COAL ONLY LARCE

ED M.965 M.554 BXS

PETROLEUM CREOSOTE X A

LOCO SAND LOCO COAL LOCO ASHES

MOTOR CAR VAN STORES SLEEPERS

GUNPOWDER VAN OIL-CAS HOLDER

CALF VAN ENCINEER'S DEPARTMENT MEDIUM

SIGNAL DEP.T STORES DEP.T BALLAST BRAKE

REFRIGERATOR MEAT VAN

To carry 6 tons Passenger Trains and 8 tons Goods Trains   *To be returned to LEICESTER*   *To be returned to ALEXANDRA DOCK LIVERPOOL*

To be returned to BURTON   *To be returned to Carlisle*   *To carry 5 Tons on Passenger Trains " " 6 Tons by Goods Trains*   *12 Ton Girder Wagon*

Copyright drawings 1978 by P.G. Chatham (P.C. Models). No reproduction without prior written permission.

Figure 29

Chapter 3 Open Wagons-Goods and Mineral

In 1923, when Midland practice was largely adopted by the L.M.S., open wagons were then divided into goods or mineral rather than goods and mineral and it is the original Midland Railway Classification which has caused the author to group them all into one large opening chapter. Indeed if these volumes were to be based upon percentages of types used and numbers thereof, then this chapter would comprise well over half the work. In some respect there is a degree of overlap between Chapter 3 and Chapter 4 but the division seemed to suggest that if it was an open wagon which carried goods or mineral it should be Chapter 3 and if it was any other type of open vehicle it should be Chapter 4, with the exception of those which were classified as specials! Such are the problems for railway historians when classifying freight rolling stock.

In this chapter we will consider a number of types covered by several diagrams together with examples of these types built before and perhaps scrapped before the final Midland Railway diagram book was issued.

Low Goods Wagons Diagram 305—Fig. 30.

During the pre-1877 period a number of drawings were issued and described as 'low sided' and examples of early construction will be found in Chapter 1. However, the first drawing to be issued after 1877 was No. 213 in that year. It is summarized below.

Drawing No.	Lot.	Qty.	Date	Remarks
213	6	500	1877	
	54	1000	1880	
	66	1000	1881	(with new type brakes)
	84	1000	1882	
	134	1000	1885	
	164	250	1887	
Total		4750		

An additional 500 were constructed in 1878 to drawing No. 216, making a grand total of 5250, 6 ton low side goods wagons whose life in traffic should have extended until c1910–1920.

There followed a gap of 10 years until 1897 when a new drawing for 8 ton low side wagons was issued and vehicles built to drawing No. 1143 are summarized below.

Drawing No.	Lot.	Qty.	Date
1143	394	1000	1897
	448	500	1898
	631	100	1905
	636	2500	1905
	682	1000	1907
Total		5100	

Life in traffic until c1930–1947.

These were very similar to drawing 213, the difference being in the internal buffer spring arrangements, continuous drawgear and a 'stop' at the ends of the sides.

A new drawing was issued in 1909 described as 'similar to drawing 1143 except brakes' and construction was as follows:—

Drawing No.	Lot.	Qty.	Date
3208	718	500	1909
	736	500	1909
	747	500	1910
	751	500	1910
	772	500	1911
	785	250	1911
	798	250	1912
	809	250	1912
	814	250	1912
	891	250	1914
	901	250	1915
Total		4000	

Life in traffic until c1939-1950.

A final drawing was issued in 1915 and a new diagram, number 818, was issued to cover wagons constructed and the summary is as below. **Fig. 33**.

Drawing No.	Lot	Qty.	Date
4340	905	350	1915
	915	200	1916
Total		550	

For some reason the wagons built to lot 915 were shown as being 8 ton and it is possible that they were fitted with 8" x 3½" journals, as per diagram 305, and not 9" x 3¾" as per the new diagram. Most certainly they would have lasted until c1950, after which date Midland wagons that were still in existence, began to vanish rapidly. Nevertheless, examples of low side Midland wagons survived into the 1960's, in departmental use, and running in private ownership; for example The Port of Bristol Authority, Bass Brewery, etc.

Naturally, wagons built to a similar design, over a long period of time, and subjected to rebuilding and modification over a span of more than eighty years, cannot be described in a few words; nor does numbering and livery detail, so necessary for modellers, make easy or simple reading. However, an attempt will be made to summarise the changes over the years.

When first constructed, all wagons built to drawing 213 were fitted with grease axleboxes, single side brakes, as per **Plate 68**, wagon No. 5044 shown in the original livery as built to lot 84. No other photographs are known to exist for vehicles built to this drawing which show running numbers.

Construction of wagons to drawing 1143 were as vehicle No. 10282, **Plate 69**—an example of lot 394 as running c1898. Apart from M.R. we now have double vee hangers and 'stop' blocks at the end of the sides.

It is believed that grease boxes were fitted to all vehicles built to drawing 1143, and that those built to drawing 3208 received oil boxes from new. However, many wagons constructed prior to 1909 later received oil axle boxes.

The wagons built to drawings 213, 216 and 1143 were originally fitted with brakes on one side only and, indeed, the very early batches were equipped with wooden brake blocks. It is not certain when the change from one to two vee hangers was made; probably with vehicles built new to drawing 1143. From c1911, wagons had to have brakes on both sides, with the lever to the right of a man facing the vehicle. Some vehicles received 'both side brakes' with the levers both at the same end, see **Plate 71** wagon No. 2244 as running c1936. Because the original Board of Trade regulations regarding both side brakes allowed twenty years' grace to Companies owning more than 20,000 wagons, many were scrapped without being altered. An extension for a further seven years enabled many more to escape alterations, and so it has been necessary to illustrate these variations by use of photograph and captions.

Other variations concerned the spring controller arrangement on the sides (see close-up **Plate 74**). This could be one only (see **Plate 81**) or two, or none at all, or a wooden block, (see **Plate 78**). Not even the length of the brake lever helps. In general, pre drawing 3208 should be a short lever and drawing 3208 vehicles should have a long brake lever. However, **Plate 78** (wagon No. 6716) shows a long brake lever with grease axleboxes, so if the axleboxes are original, it was almost certainly an example of drawing 1143. If it is an example of drawing 3208 construction with the correct brake lever, then it really should not have grease axleboxes!

The full story behind drawing 4340 (D818) is told in Chapter 1 page 25, but, briefly, it was decided to construct future low goods to the 16' 6" standard headstock length, rather than the old 14' 11". Examples of these longer lowside goods wagons are illustrated on **Plates 81 and 82**.

Apart from their use in revenue traffic, many were used as ballast wagons or for Engineering Department work, and these are illustrated and described on **Plates 83–87**. Their livery in engineering department work was red oxide, not the grey of traffic vehicles. However, all basic livery information is given in Chapter 2.

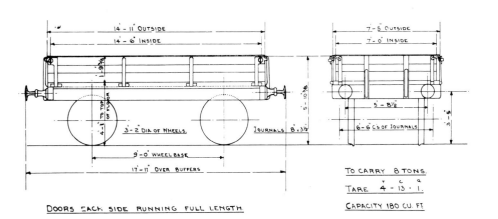

Figure 30

D305

8 TON LOWSIDED GOODS WAGON.

DOORS EACH SIDE RUNNING FULL LENGTH.

TO CARRY 8 TONS.
TARE 4 - 13 - 1.
CAPACITY 180 CU. FT.

Figures **31 and 32** are 4 mm scale drawing of the 1874 and 1882 design of low good wagon and principally illustrate the variations in brake gear.

Drawn by G.N.I. Ibbo

Plate 68 wagon No. 5044 to lot 84 original condition. 8A grease axlebo single side brake gear, no lettering oth than the cast number plate emphasis the c1883 appearance.

Photograph British R

Plate 69 illustrates c1898 constructi to lot 394. Compare with wagon N 5044, **Plate 68**. Open not solid spoke double not single vee hanger, reverse position for numberplate and 'M.R.' bodyside.

Photograph British R

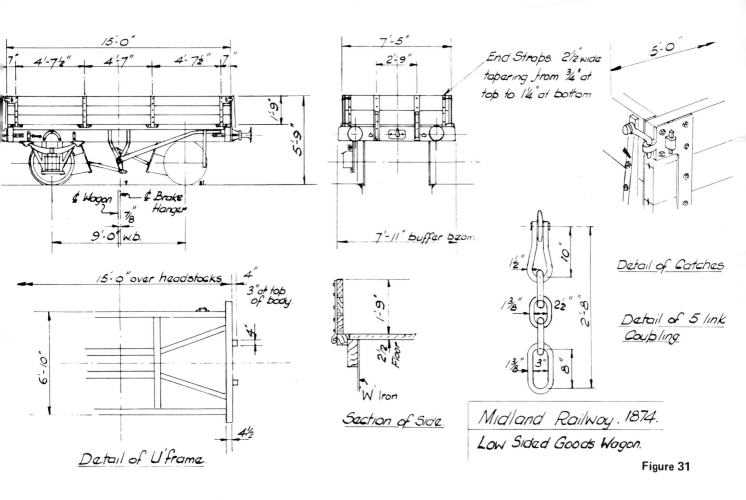

15'·0"

7" 4'·7½" 4'·7" 4'·7½" 7"

7'·5"

2'·9"

End Straps. 2½"wide tapering from ¾" at top to 1¼" at bottom

5'·0"

1'·9"

5'·9"

¢ Wagon ¢ Brake Hanger

⅞"

9'·0" w.b.

7'·11" buffer beam

Detail of Catches

1½"

10"

Detail of 5 link Coupling

1⅜"

2½"

2'·8"

1⅜"

3"

8"

15'·0" over headstocks

4"

3" at top of body

6'·10"

4"

4½"

Detail of U'frame.

1'·9"

2½" Floor

W' Iron

Section of Side.

Midland Railway. 1874.

Low Sided Goods Wagon.

Figure 31

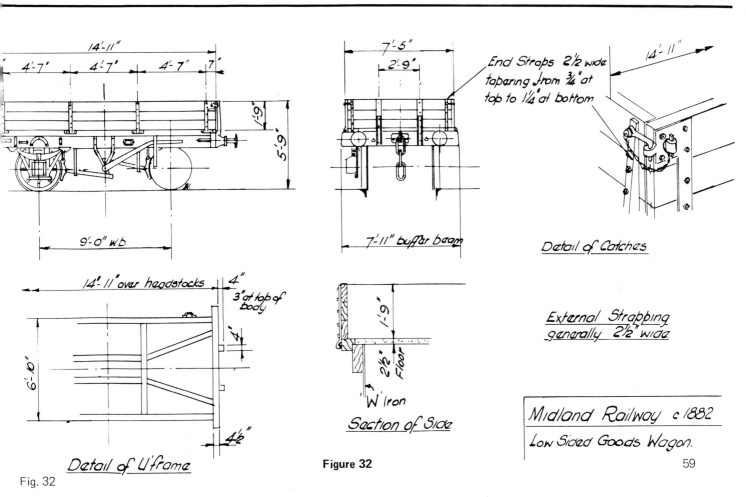

14'·11"

4'·7" 4'·7' 4'·7" 7'

7'·5"

2'·9"

End Straps 2½" wide tapering from ¾" at top to 1¼" at bottom

14'·11"

1'·9"

5'·9"

9'·0" w.b.

7'·11" buffer beam

Detail of Catches

14'·11" over headstocks

4"

3" at top of body

6'·10"

4"

4½"

Detail of U'frame

1'·9"

2½" Floor

'W' Iron

Section of Side

External Strapping generally 2½" wide

Midland Railway c 1882

Low Sided Goods Wagon.

Figure 32

Fig. 32

59

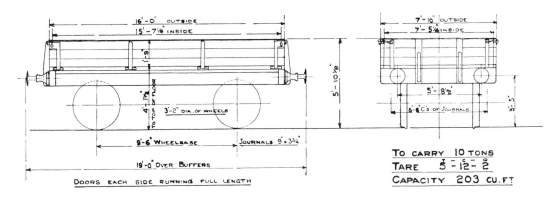

Figure 33

To carry 10 tons
TARE 5 - 12 - 2
CAPACITY 203 cu. ft

DOORS EACH SIDE RUNNING FULL LENGTH

D 818
10 TON LOWSIDED GOODS WAGON

Plate 70

M R
79 SACKS 7.18
LOCKED LOAD.
MIDLAND
119497
412

M S
2244 4

Plate 71

3229.

Plate 72 illustrates wagon No. 16600 of lot 636, just re-painted in early L.M.S. livery. Brake levers both at 'one end', grease axleboxes, end blocks only.

Photograph British Rail

◀ **Plate 70** illustrates M.R. wagon No. 119497. This vehicle was part of lot 448 and was photographed to illustrate a 'locked load' of sacks prior to the tarpaulin sheet being placed over the load. End blocks only, grease axleboxes, single side brakes.

Photograph British Rail

◀ **Plate 71** shows wagon No. 2244 as running c1936, with both brake levers at the same end. Centre wooden block, oil axleboxes, pre-1936 L.M.S. livery.

Photograph G. Y. Hemmingway

Plate 72a Midland Railway Hereford–Brecon freight train at Talyllyn Junction, Brecon & Merthyr Railway, c1892–3 0-6-0 No. 707 (later No. 2599).

George Dow Collection

Plate 73

Plates 73 and 74 illustrate wagon No. DM17634 as running in 1966 with oil axleboxes, short brake lever, double counter balance, inside vee hanger.
Photograph Author's Collection

Plate 74

Plate 75 illustrates wagon No. 658 with short brake levers, oil axleboxes, end blocks only. Note 'inside vee hanger only'.
Photograph G. Y. Hemmingway

Plate 75

Plate 76

Plate 76 illustrates M.R. wagon No. 17?15 in M.R. livery and clearly shows how barrels were loaded and roped onto low goods wagons. Note oil axleboxes, double spring controller, long brake lever and one side brakes.

Photograph British Rail

Plate 77 is wagon No. 11440 in L.M.S. livery c1936. Oil axleboxes, long brake lever, two spring controllers.

Photograph G.Y. Hemmingway

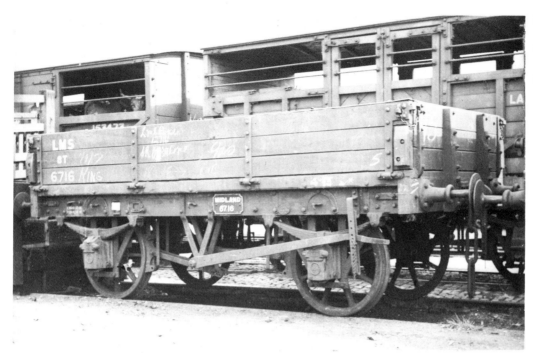

Plate 78 illustrates a wagon in post-1936 livery. Wagon No. 6716 has grease axleboxes, long brake lever and end blocks only.

Photograph A.E. West

Plate 79 shows wagon No. 26818 in early L.M.S. grey but with post-1936 numbering style, photographed c1939. A number of wagons were re-lettered in the new 1936 style without the bodywork being repainted.

Photograph A.E. West

Plate 80 illustrates B.R. 'livery' of unpainted body, M17540 as running on 22 August, 1953. It was built in 1914 to lot 891 and shows oil axleboxes, long brake lever and double spring controller.

Photograph A.E. West

Plate 81 This is an example of D818 wagon No. 110289. Note the single spring controller, oil axlebox and long brake lever.

Photograph British Rail

Plate 82 This is another example of D818. The original number was not known. At the time it was photographed at Horwich in 1964 it was 021573 and it is not known when the disc wheels were fitted. Attention is drawn to the double spring controller compared with the single spring controller in **Plate 81**.

Photograph Author's Collection

Plate 83 Photographed at St. Albans (pre 1907) it shows a train in Engineers livery with large E.D's. Note the canvas shield over the axlebox, wooden brakes on some, and no brakes visible on other vehicles.

Photograph Loco & General

Plates 83—87 illustrate examples in departmental stock.

Plate 84 illustrates wagon No. 10077 in a similar condition to the vehicles in **Plate 83**. It appears to be loaded with small scrap iron. The canvas shield over the axleboxes is clearly visible.

Photograph Author's Collection

Plate 85 This wagon was photographed in ▶ 1934 and on the original print it was branded, 'Walsall' in a similar manner to **Plate 87**. However, no running number is visible and the number plate is not clear.

Photograph R.E. Lacy

Plate 86 illustrates wagon No. 11442 as ▶ running in 1939. Note the branding variation compared with **Plate 87**.

Photograph A.E. West

Plate 87 illustrates wagon No. 4795 ▶ allocated to Manchester. All these E.D. Wagons were probably painted red oxide and all have grease axleboxes.

Photograph Author's Collection

Plate 85

Other examples not illustrated but noted in Department Stock were No. 10884 branded 'Loco Sand' in block script, and an unknown wagon branded 'L.M.S. Loco Ashes', all in block script.

Both these examples were probably in grey livery.

This completes 'ED' Wagon information.

Plate 86

Plate 87

Plate 88

Plate 89

Finally **Plates 88 & 89** illustrate wagons still running but not in railway service. Port of Bristol Authority wagon No. 136 was photographed at Avonmouth in 1963 while **Plate 89** is Bass No. 26 which carried a Derby 1902 plate. It has acquired new end stanchions to support the rounded ends.

Photograph Plate No. 88 C.M. Strevens
Plate No. 89 Author's Collection

NUMBERING DETAILS D305

The variations of axlebox, brakes and door stops are most confusing and the following information has been compiled to assist modellers. All vee hangers are double, unless noted and both side: some wagons had two sets of independent brakes, some only had the brake blocks on one side, with brake levers both sides.

Tare weight in brackets, when known.
Brake lever short   Axlebox Oil   Centre Wooden Block only
12447 (4.12), 13615*,   102005
Brake lever both at same end. Otherwise as above.
2244 (4.10)
Brake lever short   Axlebox Oil   End Blocks only
3006*† 32740*
Brake lever short   One side only,   Axlebox Grease, End Blocks only
10884 (Loco Sand)   119497 (4.12) 9563 (4.14)
Brake lever short   Axlebox Oil   End Blocks only
658 (5.2)*   17575
Brake lever short   Axlebox Grease   End Blocks only
6716 (4.13) 9490 (4.12) 16600 (4.16)* 119058
Brake lever long   Axlebox Oil   End Blocks only
26818 (4.16)
Brake lever long   Axlebox Oil   Single spring controller
34387 (4.17), 62341 (5.2)
Brake lever short   Axlebox Oil   Double spring controller
17634 (4.10)*, 22535*
Brake lever long   Axlebox Oil   Double spring controller
111 (4.14), 3354 (4.14), 7770 (4.13), 11440 (4.14.2)
17437, 17540, 18242 (4.17), 19051, 20749 (4.11.), 23948 (4.14), 25869 (4.14), 30561 (5.1.3), 52088 (4.14), 73500 (5.1.)
Brake lever long   Axlebox Grease   Double spring controller
93786

* Inside vee hanger
† Both brake levers at the same end.

Numbering Details D818
110289 (**Plate 81**).

HIGH SIDED GOODS WAGONS

In this chapter, a high-sided wagon is one which has five or more planks or where the height of the side from floor to top of the side, exceeds 2' 10". Several diagrams meet this requirement but, if we narrow the choice to read between 2' 10" and 3' 2" from floor to top of the side and to have five planks then we have a batch of vehicles, which bear a family likeness and which, with one exception, were principally built for merchandise traffic. A summary of these wagons by diagram No. and building date reads as below:-

Drawing No.	Lot	Qty.	Date
402	29	1000	1879 similar to D299

Plate 90 illustrates wagon No. 29350 built at Derby in 1875 and which is basically D299 but with a through top plank. Note the straight not 'J' shaped strapping by the side of the door, single vee hanger, long straight brake handle narrow body—see protruding headstock. The numberplate is interesting, the numbers are smaller than on later wagons (see **Plates 91 and 92**.)

Photograph British Rail

Plate 91 is a vehicle from lot 29. Wagon No. 31449 was built to drawing 402 in 1880 and has a tare of 4.18.1. The 'J' strapping is now in evidence and, unlike **Plate 92**, this vehicle has an early form of doorstop. Note five link couplings and wooden brake blocks. Also note narrower body when compared with D299 vehicles.

Photograph British Rail

Plate 91

Both these wagons pre-date D299, see **Plates 92—98**, but it is not possible to say just when this style of high goods wagon was introduced. The only other high goods recorded comes from an earlier period, see **Plate 30 and Plate 34**.

Plate 92 photographed in 1894 is a typical D299 wagon. Large 'M.R' single side brake, with double vee hangers; all that is missing is the later door stop. This wagon has a small square plate which is attached to the side where it falls against the vee hanger.

Photograph British Rail

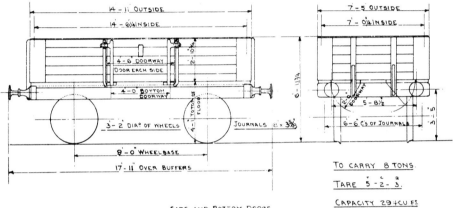

Diagram 299 Figure 34

——— 8 TON HIGH-SIDED WAGON. ——

Drawing No.	Lot	Qty.	Date
550	82	2000	1882
	115	2000	1884
	135	4000	1885
	160	1000	1886
	178	2000	1887
	196	2000	1887
	207	1000	1888
	217	3000	1888
	232	4000	1889
	252	5000	1890
	281	6000	1891
	298	1000	1892
	306	4000	1892
	327	4000	1893
	343	5000	1894
	358	2000	1895
	382	2000	1896
	423	3000	1897
	461	3000	1899
	483	4000	1899
	513	2000	1899
	632	10	1905
	919	1000	1917 similar to lot 632
Total	...	63,010	

All were built with bottom doors, the lot book describing each lot in terms of 'As Before', except lot 919 which was described as 'Similar to lot 632' and is probably explained by the fact that lot 919 had both side brakes, whereas the remainder were built with 'One side brakes'.

Diagram 300 Fig. 35, is something of a mystery in that no record appears to exist for them. The author's view is that some vehicles were so altered from D299 but, how many and when, is not known. Probably, only a very small number pre the construction of the wagons built to D304.

Unlike the later diagrams, D299 was for both goods and mineral and many were used for loco coal traffic. Although far more numerous than D305 low goods wagons, their active life was less. Apart from lot 919, scrapping would have begun c1910—20 and large numbers were withdrawn during the 1920's without the brakegear being altered. The L.M.S. built almost 60,000 12 ton merchandise wagons 1923—30 and in so doing replaced most of the Midland vehicles. However, some survived until c1939, but it is unlikely that any were running in 1945, apart from possible examples in department stock. They were, however, the most numerous class of wagon built by any railway company pre 1948 and almost every railway scene pre 1923 could have included one or more examples of this class.

It is difficult to understand why lot 919 was built to drawing 550 in 1917, four years after construction of D302

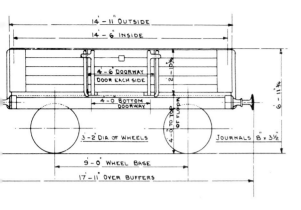

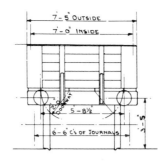

Figure 35

D300

TO CARRY 8 TONS.
TARE 5 - 3 - 3.
CAPACITY 293 CU FT
(PG)
—— 8 TON HIGH-SIDED WAGON ——

SIDE AND BOTTOM DOORS.

FITTED WITH THE AUTOMATIC VACUUM THROUGH PIPE.

commenced and twelve years after the
ious building of wagons to this early draw-
One possible solution is that it was to use
aterial on hand for other 14' 11" wagons,
this is far from certain. What is certain,
ever, is that drawing 550 was used and this
ified drawing which now shows oil axle-
es together with both side brakes and a
r brake handle to that which appears in
es **92—98** which illustrate the early con-
tion. In view of the date of building, the
lever was more like the type used in D302
this, together with vertical strapping located
way between the doors and corner plates,
ars on the drawing. It would seem, there-
that 1,000 wagons were so built and they
until the 1940's. However, these vehicles
ost elusive and have almost defied attempts
ace any running numbers.

Plate 93

Plate 94

Plates 93 and 94 have been selected to
illustrate D299 vehicles and while their
basic condition is similar, **Plate 93**, wagon
No. 34350 has the running number painted
on the bodyside and its livery is identical
to wagon No. 124124, **Plate 94**. It is interesting to note that No. 34350 has both
side brake gear. Wagon No. 124124 has
been included in order to illustrate the
method for loading sacks into an open
wagon.

Both Photographs British Rail

71

Plate 95 This is two for the price of one! Some wagons to D299 were used for loco coal traffic and while livery styles varied with later diagrams photographic evidence suggests that D299 were liveried accordingly. No photos are known to exist showing L.M.S. livery in loco coal traffic.

Photograph Author's Collection

Plate 96 Taken in 1936 it illustrates wagon No. 79102 in L.M.S. livery. Pictures in L.M.S. livery are rare and here we have a Midland wagon still with one side brakes. Note the later style of door stop.

This selection of plates of D299 type wagons illustrates their livery very clearly. Very little variation in style for such a large number of wagons.

Photograph G. Y. Hemmingway

Plate 97 The illustration of wagon No. 121107 is something of a mystery. The vehicle is part of lot 513 and was built in 1901, but why the light coloured triangle and numberplate?

The colour of the triangle appears to be yellow and this 'style' is unknown to the author on any other vehicle.

Photograph British Rail

e **98** is an accident picture pre 1907
the wagon number is 50180. Apart
n illustrating the end detail, it also
trates the chalk number 6 which was
there by the shunter to indicate to his
w shunters into which siding the
on was to be shunted.

Photograph British Rail

e **99** is one of the two known photo-
hs of wagons to lot 919 of D299 and
photographed in c1936 illustrating
on No. 75036.

Photograph G.Y. Hemmingway

The logical development of D299 appeared in 1913 with
an increase of 1' 0'' over the previous design over headstocks, 6'' longer wheelbase and 4'' overbody width and
they were classified as **diagram 302**—10 ton high-sided
wagon **Fig. 36**.

Diagram 302   Fig. 36

Drawing No.	Lot	Qty.	Date	
3843	825	250	1913	
	864	500	1914	
	871	500	1914	
	899	500	1915	
	910	500	1916	
	917	500	1916	
	929	1000	1918	
	935	1000	1918	
	940	1000	1919	
	943	1000	1920	
	948	1000	1920	700 10-ton side & bottom doors, 200 12-ton side & bottom doors, 100 12-ton side doors.
	953	1000	1920	
	954	1000	1920	925 x 12 ton 75 x 10 ton
Total		9750		

Figure 36

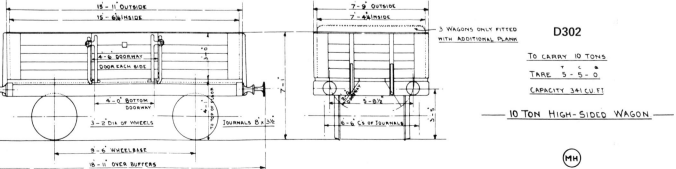

D302

TO CARRY 10 TONS

TARE 5 - 5 - 0

CAPACITY 341 CU. FT

— 10 TON HIGH-SIDED WAGON —

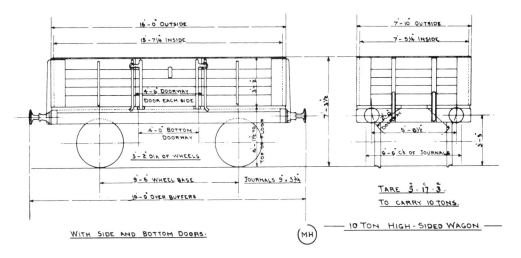

With side and bottom doors.

10 TON HIGH-SIDED WAGON

TARE 5.17.3.
TO CARRY 10 TONS.

Figure 37

D663A

Apart from lot 953, all were built with side and bottom doors. This diagram led to the final Midland design to appear in Midland livery, and even then, some were too late to carry 'M.R.' and left Derby in L.M.S. livery, which was really M.R. grey with L.M.S. on the side, replacing the M.R. No other changes in livery styles taking place when originally constructed. They remained in traffic until c1950.

D663A   Figure 37

Drawing No.	Lot	Qty.	Date
5279	956	1000	1921
	957	1000	1921
	976	500	1922
	986	500	1922
	1000	500	1923
Total		3500	

The difference from D302 vehicles was 1″ extra in length, 2″ extra in height and 9″ x 3¾″ journals, compared with 8″ x 3½″, and 1″ extra in width. The principal change was visually in that the end posts of D302 were wooden while those of D663A were steel T Section. D663A was in traffic until c1955.

Plate 100 illustrates D302 wagon No. 93166 from lot 823 built in April 1913. By now we have oil axleboxes, both side brakes but the family likeness from the 1870's is still to be seen.

Photograph British Rail

Plate 101 illustrates wagon No. 20261 in early L.M.S. grey livery. Photographed c1936 the M.R. can still be seen showing through.

Photograph G.Y. Hemmingway

Plate 102 illustrates wagon No. 93792 in a rare L.M.S. wagon livery. The wagon was built in 1921 and is either lot 953 or 954 and was photographed at Aylesbury on the 5th May, 1939. The livery is grey but the lettering is in the style and location normally associated with the bauxite livery introduced in 1936. Some new L.M.S. construction carried the small L.M.S. on grey livery but it is very rare on old wagons.

Note: Disc wheels—somewhat uncommon for this class of vehicle.

Photograph A.J. Watson

Plate 103 illustrates D302 in B.R. days. M19950 is in 'Unpainted' livery with dark patches onto which the numbering details have been painted.

Photograph R. England

D663A WAGONS

Plates **104–106** are all of D663A—the final M.R. open goods design to appear during Midland Railway ownership and even so many, built in 1923, were liveried L.M.S. from new—see frontispiece.

Plate 104 photographed c1936 clearly shows M.R. some thirteen years after the company ceased to exist—the wagon number appears to be 11877 and is only to be found on the cast numberplate.

Photograph G.Y. Hemmingway

Plate 105 wagon No. 83721 never carried M.R. livery. This vehicle was built new in 1923 and is in 'M.R.' livery with L.M.S. replacing the M.R. Note the T end stanchion which is the principal difference between D663A and D302 vehicles.

Photograph British Rail

Plate 104

In 1923 to drawing 5612, Midland Railway lot 100[?] 1000 new design wagons appeared. Later to be known a[s] diagram 1666, this was the L.M.S. standard design and so from 1882 until 1930, the family born from drawing 55[?] multiplied to more than 125,000 wagons, which must con[?] stitute a record for freight rolling stock in the Unite[d] Kingdom, perhaps even the world. However, there wer[e] three variations of the D299 theme and two of these varia[?] tions are dealt with in this chapter.

Plate 105

Plate 106 This picture illustrates wagon No. 17071 in South Wales c1936. Traces of M.R. are still visible with a few traces of grey paint but recently the wagon number has been renewed.

Photograph G.Y. Hemmingway

Plate 107 Finally, illustrates wagon No. 6469 in post-1936 bauxite livery, photographed in December 1946.

Photograph H.C. Casserley

Fig. No. 38
This drawing was produced from general arrangement drawing 5279 and illustrates the vehicle built to D663A.

Drawing M. Peascod

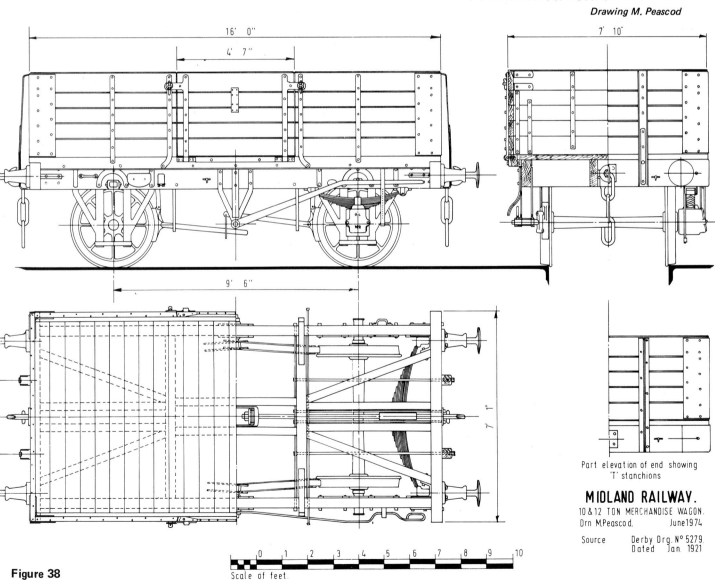

Part elevation of end showing 'T' stanchions

MIDLAND RAILWAY.
10 & 12 TON MERCHANDISE WAGON.
Drn M.Peascod.   June 1974

Source   Derby Drg. N° 5279.
          Dated Jan. 1921

Figure 38

Scale of feet.

Plate 108

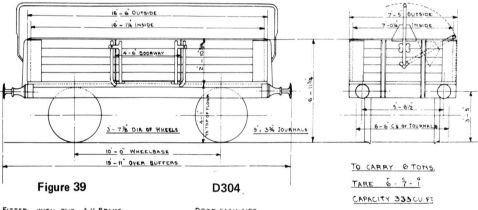

Figure 39   **D304**

FITTED WITH THE A.V. BRAKE
COMPLETE AND THE HAND BRAKE.

DOOR EACH SIDE.

TO CARRY 6 TONS.
TARE 6 - 5 - 9
CAPACITY 333 CU FT

— BISCUIT WAGON. —

D304 Biscuit Wagon

Drawing No. 2820

Lot	Qty	Date
669	10	1907 for Carrs Biscuit traffic

Probably ran in traffic until c1935

The 10 wagons to D304 were built to convey Carrs Biscuits from Carlisle and the use of an open wagon with a tarpaulin bar for this traffic is interesting. It is not known how long they were used for this traffic. They did, however, remain in service until the mid-1930's.

Plates 108 and 109 illustrate the biscuit wagon D304 and are the only two pictures known to the author. The picture of wagon No. 65721 is in the original 1908 livery and the legend at the right hand end reads 'To work between Carlisle and Leyton'.

Photograph British Rail

Plate 109 is of wagon No. 67824, taken some years later and there appears to be no visible evidence of ownership. It is interesting in that these were the only Midland wagons to be equipped with a tarpaulin sheet bar. Later, in M.R. and presumably, L.M.S. days, a large 'X' appeared on the door.

Photograph Author's Collection

Plate 109

D351 END DOOR WAGONS

Plates 110–112 illustrate D351, which was the end door version of **D299. Plate 110** of wagon No. 100000 shows an 1890 livery of a wagon belonging to lot 244 and clearly illustrates the 'No Brake Side'. An almost similar viewpoint is pictured in **Plate 111** of wagon No. 105563 which has been subjected to a 'Rough Shunt'. As a result, the load has moved and burst open the end door.

Both Photographs British Rail

Plate 110

Plate 111

Plate 112 shows wagon No. 123984 in an interesting livery. The size and position of the numbers and L.M.S. suggest the post 1936 bauxite livery, but for this livery, one would have expected the white stripe to be on the diagonal strapping, as used on the standard L.M.S. 12-ton minerals. However, it is probably in bauxite and was photographed in 1939.

Photograph A.J. Watson

Diagram 351 - 8 ton high-sided wagon with side, end and bottom doors. See Figures 40 & 41.

Drawing No.	Lot	Qty.	Date
790	244	1000	1890
	285	500	1891
	319	500	1893
	378	500	1896
	405	2500	1897
	427	2000	1897
	490	2000	1900
Total		9000	

Probably ran in traffic until c1945

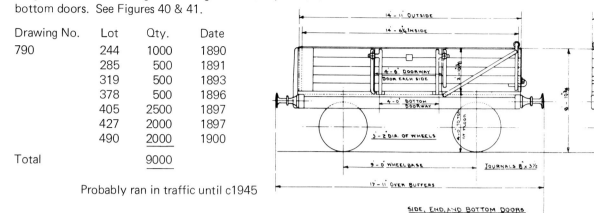

SIDE, END, AND BOTTOM DOORS

D351

Figure 40

8 TON HIGHSIDED WAGON.

D351 was described as "end door" and almost certainly always used for coal traffic and they lead the reader into the realms of even higher sided wagons, which were largely used for mineral traffic.

The earliest design of higher sided wagon was the coke wagon and only one diagram, No. 342, was issued, using drawing 760. However, prior to this, 50 vehicles were built to drawing 358. A full summary of coke wagons is given below:-

No diagram issued.

Drawing No.	Lot	Qty.	Date
358	15	50	1878

Almost certainly non-existent by 1918

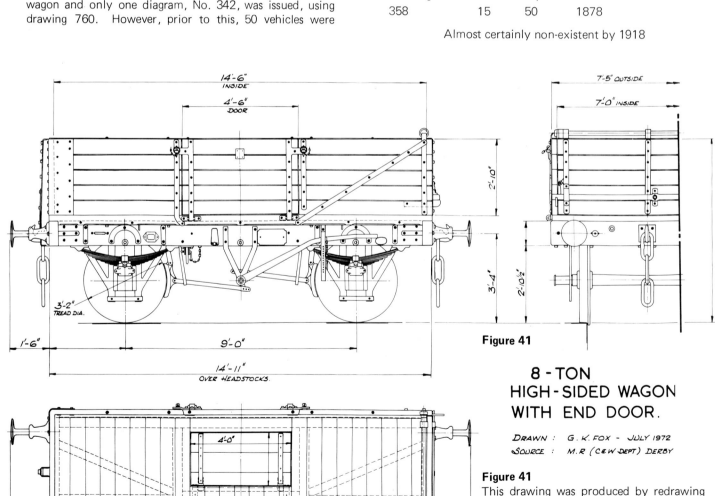

Figure 41

8 - TON
HIGH - SIDED WAGON
WITH END DOOR.

DRAWN : G. K. FOX - JULY 1972
SOURCE : M.R (C&W DEPT) DERBY

Figure 41
This drawing was produced by redrawing general arrangement drawing 790.

G.K. Fox

Diagram 342—Figure 42

Drawing No.	Lot	Qty.	Date
760	218	1	1888
	221	1000	1889
	317	300	1893
	347	250	1894
	390	250	1896
	457	25	1899
	491	500	1900
	768	50	1911
	784	50	1911
	813	50	1912
Total		2476	

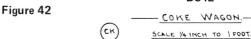

The lot book states that lots 317–813 were built with bottom doors, but the diagram book suggests that only 1325 were so equipped.

Some vehicles survived until c1940 but it is doubtful if many received the bauxite livery introduced in 1936.

During the same year which saw the introduction of the first type of coke wagon, the Midland Railway introduced hopper bottom wagons to drawing 682, later allocated to diagram 343, construction details on page 84.

Figure 42

D342

(CK)   COKE WAGON.

SCALE ¼ INCH TO 1 FOOT.

TO CARRY 8 TONS.
TARE 5 - 5 - 1.
CAPACITY 580 CU.FT

NOTE.—1325 OF THESE WAGONS ARE FITTED WITH BOTTOM DOORS SIMILAR TO THE 8, 10, & 12 TON HIGHSIDED WAGONS.

This note suggests that the diagram book, from which Fig. 42 was made, was published between lots 491 and 768 being introduced.

Plate 113 illustrating coke wagon No. 1947 is an example of lot 15 built in 1879 and, as can clearly be seen, is the precursor of the familiar and distinctive Midland vehicle which lasted into the 1940's. It carried all the features from this period, five link couplings, wooden brake blocks. No visible livery except the cast number plate. See also **Plate No. 7.**

Photograph British Rail

Plate 114 is a poor photograph but has been included for its historical value. The date is unknown except that it is post-1890. The appearance of a coke wagon to D342 confirms this point but, clearly evident, is a high-sided wagon, ten planks high with modern diagonal strapping and cupboard doors. It has wooden brake blocks and dumb buffers and, almost certainly, is a private owner wagon taken over by the Midland Railway, as described in Chapter 1.

Photograph British Rail

81

Plates **115—117** illustrate D342 in various guises.

Plate 115 showing wagon No. 59472 is an example of lot 221 in original condition with one side brakes.

Photograph British Rail

Plate 116 shows wagon No. 90050 taken in May 1939 clearly illustrating pre-1936 L.M.S. livery even to the extent of the 'N', Non Common User markings. By now both side brakes have been acquired.

Photograph A.J. Watson

Plate 117 illustrates wagon No. 100410 which is a rare example of a coke wagon in bauxite livery. The date is October 1939 and the paint date visible on the solebar reads 19.11.37. These three pictures illustrate the liveries worn by this class of vehicle during Midland and L.M.S. ownership.

Photograph A.E. West

Midland Coal Traffic

These two pictures of Toton in 1910, have been included within this chapter to draw the reader's attention to the fact that during the period under review coal was the prime source of energy and that the Midland Railway Company was one of the principal transporters of this traffic. The marshalling yards at Toton were the focal point for the collection of loads and empties en route between the collieries and their destination and while the bulk of the traffic was carried in private owner wagons the Midland Railway owned a large number of coal wagons, all described within this chapter.

The top picture shows Toton Old Bank and the photograph was taken on the 14.2.1910. The vast majority of the wagons are private owners but there are a number of Midland wagons to be seen but, as would be expected no wagons from other railways are visible.

The bottom picture, taken on the same day, underlines the volume of coal in daily transit and this part of the yards known as Toton Meadow again shows that the majority of wagons were private owners but nevertheless a number of Midland coal wagons are evident.　　　　　　　　　　　　　　　*Both photographs British Rail, courtesy of the National Railway Museum*

HOPPER BOTTOM WAGONS

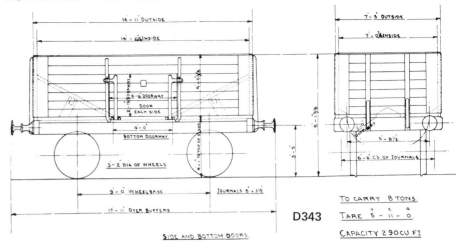

Diagram 343—Figure 43.

Drawing No.	Lot	Qty.	Date
682	200	1000	1888
	340	350	1894
	379	250	1896
	430	500	1898
Total		2100	

Figure 43

D343

TO CARRY 8 TONS
TARE 5 - 11 - 0
CAPACITY 290 CU FT

HOPPER BOTTOM WAGON.

Examples would probably have lasted until c1940

Plate 118

Plates **118/119** illustrate two examples of hopper bottom wagons to D343. **Plate 118** of wagon No. 98765 is an example of lot 200 in c1890 condition. However the black line, indicating the line of the hopper bottom, is on for photographic purposes along with the white spokes to the wheels, a feature evident on many Midland Railway official photographs.

Photograph British Rail

Plate 119 illustrates an unknown wagon of D343 and has been included to indicate the formation of the hopper bottom. Note the absence of the end vertical strapping on this vehicle compared with No. 98765.

Photograph British Rail

Plate 119

10 TON OPEN WAGONS

Other types of high sided wagons were built for goods or mineral traffic and it seems logical to consider them by date of introduction. The first to appear were 12 vehicles to drawing 1490, lot 506, in 1910 described as, '10 ton goods or coal'. No further details are known although it is possible they were similar to D301 but with a through top plank.

The same year saw the introduction of diagram 301 and the sequence of building was as below. Other construction is illustrated on pages 86—95 with a final summary of the sequence on page 96.

Diagram 301—Figure 44

Drawing No.	Lot	Qty.	Date
1530	529	1000	1901
	530	80	1902 Built for S&DJR
Total		1000 + 80 built	

Plate 120 shows wagon No. 120655 in pre-1936 L.M.S. livery. This class seemed to have evaded photographers and this is the only photograph known to exist in M.R. or L.M.S. livery. On the other hand **Plate 121** shows an example of lot 530 and is S&DJR wagon No. 1179, one of eighty vehicles built for this railway at Derby. Wagon No. 1179 is without a door stop, wagon No. 120655 has one otherwise they appear to be identical.

Both Photographs British Rail

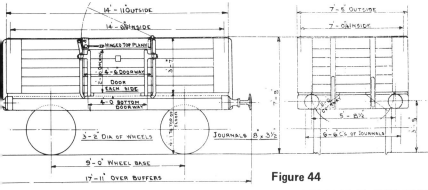

Figure 44

D301

TO CARRY 10 TONS.

TARE 5 - 5 - 3.

CAPACITY 366 CU FT

—— 10 TON HIGHSIDED WAGON. -

HINGED TOP PLANK, SIDE AND BOTTOM DOORS.

Plate 121

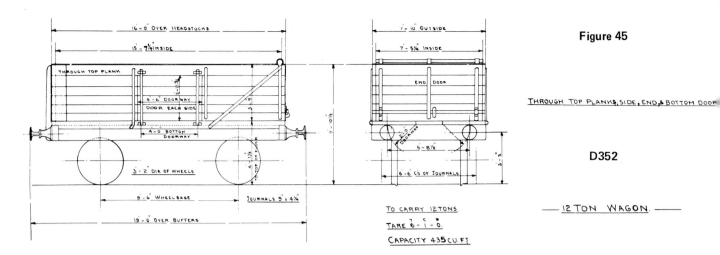

Figure 45

THROUGH TOP PLANKS, SIDE, END, & BOTTOM DOOR

D352

— 12 TON WAGON. —

TO CARRY 12 TONS.
TARE 6 - 1 - 0.
CAPACITY 435 CU. FT.

Diagram 352—Figure 45

Drawing No.	Lot	Qty.	Date
2156	Part 595	3	1904
	640	1000	1906
	676	1000	1907
	701	1000	1908
	720	1000	1909
Total		4003	

Drawing No.	Lot	Qty.	Date
2157	Part 595	3	1904 With hinged top plank

Probably as drawing 2156 except as noted.

Plates **122**—**124** illustrate D352 in various conditions.

Plate **122** shows wagon No. 84477 in original condition and calls for little comment—absolutely standard for the period of c1914.

Photograph British Rail

Plate 123 shows wagon No. 74881 in wartime condition. The small 12T L.M.S. 74881 has been painted on a 'patch' likewise the 'V'. Traces of the longer diagonal stripe and pre-1936 L.M.S. are clearly visible. The tare weight of 6.2 is painted on the corner plate.

Photograph A.G. Ellis

Plate 124 illustrating wagon No. 11719 sheeted over is again interesting from the livery standpoint. Post-1936 livery position but pre-1936 stripes. The tare of 5.19 is located on the bottom plank right hand end, a more usual location.

Photograph British Rail

Plate 123

Plate 124

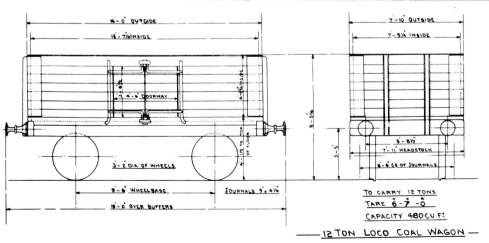

Figure 46

Diagram 204—Figure 46.

Drawing No.	Lot	Qty.
3255	731	1000
Date		
1909		

Plate 125

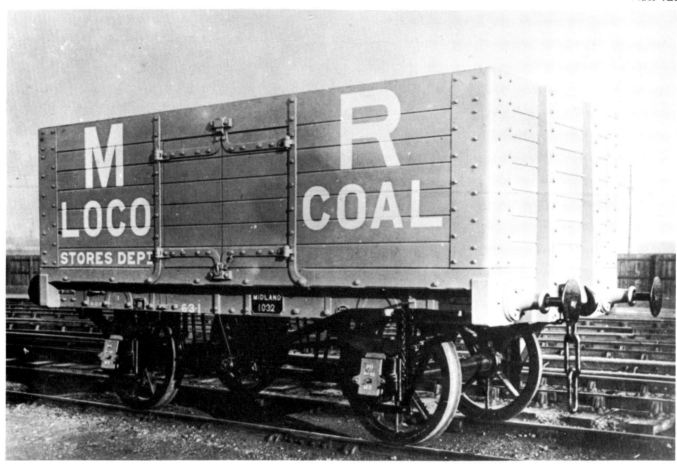

Although only 1000 vehicles were built to D204 four plates have been selected to illustrate some of the many livery conditions to be found within this class.

Plate 125 Wagon No. 1032 illustrating the original condition. some vehicles may have run without the 'Stores Dept' legend, but still branded 'Loco Coal'.

Photograph British Rail

Plate 126 showing wagon No. 71554 left and No. 70170 right c1936 clearly illustrate the difficulty in laying down rigid livery rules. Both are in grey. The left hand wagon was painted recently while the right hand wagon is much darker in colour. Perhaps economy has caused 'Loco Coal' to become 'Loco', while at the same time No. 71554 is rated 'N' (Non Common User).

Photograph G. Y. Hemmingway

Plate 126

Plate **127** showing wagon No. 95811 is most interesting. The date is post-1948 yet the original Midland livery is still evident and was chalked round prior to being photographed. There is no trace of any L.M.S. livery and this old wagon, now uprated to carry 13 tons, clearly shows c1948/9 B.R. livery and marking styles.

Photograph R. England

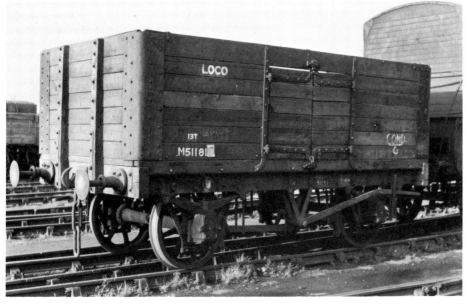

Plate **128** showing wagon No. M51181 at the end of its days in final BR livery style.

Photograph Author's Collection

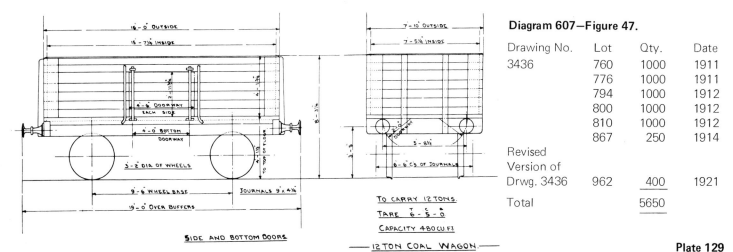

Diagram 607—Figure 47.

Drawing No.	Lot	Qty.	Date
3436	760	1000	1911
	776	1000	1911
	794	1000	1912
	800	1000	1912
	810	1000	1912
	867	250	1914
Revised Version of Drwg. 3436	962	400	1921
Total		5650	

Plate 129

Vehicles to diagram 607 also carried various livery styles and **Plates 129—137** have been selected to illustrate some of the known variations.

Plate 129 shows wagon No. 69403 in original condition and also illustrates how to load sacks.

Photograph British Rail

Plate 130 This is worthy of careful study. Wagon No. 56679 and the unidentified wagon to the right have 'Loco Coal Only' and 'M.R.' reversed, while behind No. 56679 there is another Midland wagon in a very light grey livery.

Plate 131 In pre-1936 grey livery they appear to have been lettered 'Loco Coal' as the photo of wagon No. 14372 in service but no fixed rule appears to have been applied as to the position of the 'L.M.S.' On 14372 it is closely spaced, whereas on other photographs the 'L.M.S.' was placed outside the vertical strapping.

Both photographs British Rail

Plate 130

Plate 131

91

Plate 132

Plate 133

Plate 134

Plate 132 shows wagon No. 85868 with a low 'L.M.S.' not branded for coal traffic while **Plate 133** shows wagon No. 71554 as 'Loco' 'Not in common use.'

Both Photographs G. Y. Hemmingway

A further example of the close spaced L.M.S. is evident in **Plate 134** showing wagon No. 52391, while **Plate 135** illustrates an August 1939 view of wagon No. 55410 in bauxite livery with the standard post-1936 livery style.

Plate 134 Author's Collection
Plate 135 A.E. West

Plate 135

Plate **136** shows wagon No. 72888 in wartime livery and this wagon appears to have been subject to some repairs using thinner planks on the left hand side.

Photograph Author's Collection

Plate **137** illustrates wagon No. 26333 uprated to 13T otherwise it is similar in condition to **Plate 136**.

Photograph A. Dunbar

Plate 136

Plate 137

Diagram 673—Figure 48

Was covered by both drawing 3850, lots 823—942 and drawing 5106, lots 944-999.

Lot	Qty.	Date
823	1000	1913
841	1000	1913
865	1000	1914
875	1000	1914
904	1000	1915
909	500	1916
916	500	1916
942	200	1919
944	1000	1920
949	1000	1920
999	950	1922
Total	9150	

D673

THROUGH TOP PLANKS, SIDE, END, & BOTTOM DOORS

—— 12 TON WAGON ——

Diagram 673 is covered in **Plates 138—141** and attention is drawn to wagons No. 36023 **Plate 138** and wagon No. 80957 **Plate 139**. Apart from the difference in wheels attention is drawn to the ironwork on the end door.

Both photographs British Rail

Plate 138

Plate 139

Plate 140 illustrates pre-1936 grey livery showing wagon No. 53732 carrying the broad stripe while Plate 141 illustrates wagon No. M73081 in B.R. livery with the smaller stripe. It is not possible to confirm whether the paintwork was in grey or bauxite.

Both Photographs
Author's Collection

Plate 141

Finally we come to drawing 4944 which is believed to cover D303 as below.

D303   Fig. 49.

Drawing No.	Lot	Qty.	Date
4944	936	100	1918
	937	100	1918
Total		200	

The foregoing covers the development of diagrams 301, 352, 204, 673, 303 and in summary, diagram 301 began with the retention of the 14' 11" length but in effect had an extra 9" high plank added on top of the side. It is possible that drawing 1490 was like this and then drawing 1530 authorized the change to a hinged top plank to allow easy access into the wagon. As with D299, side and bottom doors were fitted and it is interesting to note that 80 were built for the Somerset and Dorset Railway Company (see **Plate 121**).

In 1904 a change was made and drawing 2156 vehicles were classified as Diagram 352 and saw the body length increased to 16' 0" with the wheelbase now 9' 6". End doors were fitted plus side and bottom doors making this vehicle more suitable for mineral traffic. An unusual feature was the single diagonal strapping only at the end door end.

Construction ceased in 1909, the year which saw the authorization of 1000 wagons to D204, for loco coal use. An identical underframe was equipped with a side door only body with slightly higher sides. However the notable feature was the 'cupboard doors' being regarded as suitable for loco coal work. They may not have been considered a total success because in 1911 a new design—Diagram 607 appeared and construction continued over the next 10 years. The side doors for these were altered to the more conventional drop down type. There were still no end doors, but bottom doors appeared. The design was revised in 1921 for lot 962 and the drawing suggests that T end stanchions were used instead of wooden posts but regrettably no photos of this type are known to the author. Many photographs show them branded for 'Loco Coal'. This group of mineral wagons saw the introduction of another new design in 1913— D673 and construction continued until 1922/23. They were in effect D352 but with a 4¾" higher side giving a greater cubic capacity but were still rated to carry 12 tons. Unlike D352 and D607 which were principally for loco coal traffic D302 and D673 were for general mineral traffic with D301 as an odd batch of 'high goods' outside of the general development of the 5 plank high design.

The final new design to D303, consisted of 200 wagons which appeared in 1918 when two lots of 100 wagons each were authorized. The design was in effect D301 on a 16' 0" underframe instead of the 14' 11" underframe of the earlier D301 vehicles. Why 200 wagons of this type should have been built interspersed between D673 construction is not known to the author. Unfortunately no pictures are known to exist illustrating this class of vehicle.

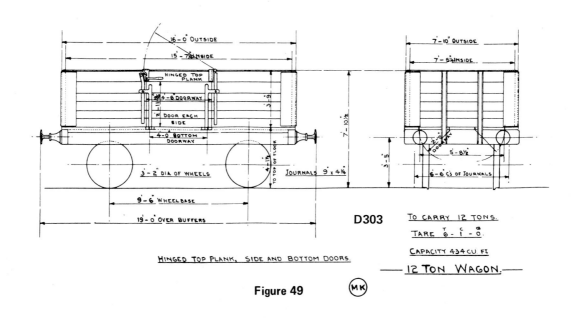

HINGED TOP PLANK, SIDE AND BOTTOM DOORS.

D303   TO CARRY 12 TONS.
TARE 6 - 1 - 0.
CAPACITY 434 CU FT
12 TON WAGON.

Figure 49

RUNNING NUMBERS

D299 8 TON HIGH SIDED WAGON

3783	22825, 24374	25222 (5.1)	29307 (4.19)
34350	35899 (4.19)	36802, 37729 (4.19.2)	39783
40757 (4.18)	41468 (4.17)	42910	43468 (4.18.2)
45211	50160 (5.0)	50180	55160 (5.1)
60311	60969, 65694 (5.0)	67137	67469
71013	71671	72532	74418 (5.1), 78114
78607	79102 (4.18.1)	79546 (5.2)	81483
83531	84119, 85357, 87237	89714 (5.3)	90569 (4.18.2)
91062 (5.3.3)	94250	97491	100406, 102048
102169	104758 (5.1.0)	104478	108146 (5.3), 110983
111936, 121107	122032 (5.0)	122767, 124024	124124, 138073 (5.2)
138978			

D299 Lot 919 75036, 96581

D300 8 TON HIGH SIDED WAGON

None recorded

D302 10 TON HIGH SIDED WAGON

16908 (5.12)	16954 (5.10)	19950 (5.16)	20261 (5.16), 24613 (5.15)
33716	62449	73055	85380
93166 (5.17.3)	93792 (6.8)	96175	111186 (5.19)

D663A 10 TON HIGH SIDED WAGON

964	4684 (5.16)	6469 (5.18), 16617	16908 (5.12)
16954 (5.10)	17071 (5.19)	17196 (5.19.2)	19665
19950 (5.16)	20261 (5.16)	23370	25075
28559	35716 (6.1.1)	36722	41595
51401	55094	55717	58196
59329 (5.17)	62449 (6.2)	65866 (6.1.1)	67716
73055	74721	76791	76879 (6.0.0)
77477 (6.6.3)	77493 (6.3.0)	81265 (5.18)	83721 (6.0.0)
85868 (6.6.0), 81265 (5.18)	86779 (6.11)	93166 (5.17.3)	91654
92478	102873	115444	126195 (5.17)

D304 BISCUIT WAGON

65721 (6.8.0)	67824

D351 8 TON HIGH SIDED WAGON

100000	105563	112534	115286
123984	126311	126774	

D342 COKE WAGON

59472 (5.4.2)	85467 (5.8.2)	90050 (5.8.0)	100410 (5 5,
104620			

D343 HOPPER BOTTOM WAGON

55903	74880	98765 (5.10.1)

D301 10 TON HIGH SIDED WAGON

120655	S&DJR 1179

D352 12 TON WAGON

11719 (5.19)	62028	65310	74881
84477	99792 (6.7.3)		

D204 12 TON LOCO COAL WAGON

1032 (6.3.1)	51181	70170 (6.2.0)	71554 (6.8.0)
93958	95811		

D607 12 TON COAL WAGON

20181 (6.2)	25988 (6.4)	26333	36116
37246	37383 (6.7)	50394	51506
52391	55410 (5.19)	56679	58170
63223	64208	64683 (6.1)	65586 (6.8)
69403	71554 (6.8.0)	72888	73420
74721	75370 (6.11)	75994	76670
80311	91022	82629 (6.2.3)	85668 (6.6.0)
86779 (6.6.1)	87540	92282 (6,0)	92892 (6.0)
93631 (6.5.0)	94775	112263	

D673 12 TON WAGON

16398 (5.19)	27471	36203 (6.10.1)	37861
53732	62028	62172	68721
69467 (6.9)	73081 (6.7)	80957 (6.9.2)	113728
111849 (6.10)			

D303 12 TON WAGON

None recorded.

15–30 TON WAGONS

The final section of this chapter deals with the larger open mineral wagons and the diagram book lists the following vehicles:—

D345   15 ton Coal Wagon Steel Body (Fig. 50)
D349   20 ton Coal Wagon Steel Body (Fig. 51)
D350   20 ton Coal Wagon Wood Body (Fig. 52)
D346   30 ton Coal Wagon Steel Body (Fig. 53)
D347   30 ton Coal Wagon Steel Body (Fig. 54)
D348   30 ton Coal Wagon Steel Body (Fig. 55)

The lot book contains no reference to D346/7/8 whatsoever. It does contain a note to the effect that drawing 3354 covered 1 wagon to lot 746 authorised on the 6th June 1910. No further details are available.

A summary of D345, D349, D350 as recorded in the lot book is given below:—

D345   15 ton Coal Wagon

Drawing No.	Lot	Qty.	Date
1757	557	5	1903

D349   20 ton Coal Wagon

Drawing No.	Lot	Qty.	Date
2802	673	175	1907 built by S. T. Claye

D350   20 ton Coal Wagon

2817	674	25	1907 built by Gloucester C & W Co. Ltd.

It is interesting to note that both lots 673/4 were authorised on the 25th July 1907 so it would seem they were constructed for comparison purposes between wood and steel wagon bodies.

Plate 142 illustrates wagon No. 2837 of D345 in original condition. Unfortunately no other photographs are known to exist.

Photograph British Rail

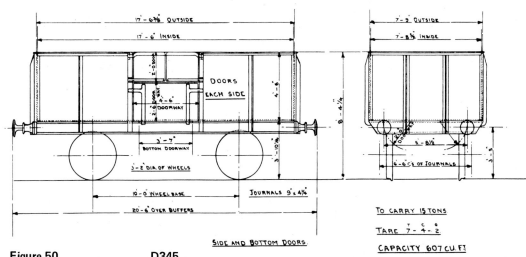

SIDE AND BOTTOM DOORS.

Figure 50   **D345**

TO CARRY 15 TONS
TARE 7 - 4 - 2
CAPACITY 607 CU. FT.
―― 15 TON COAL WAGON ――

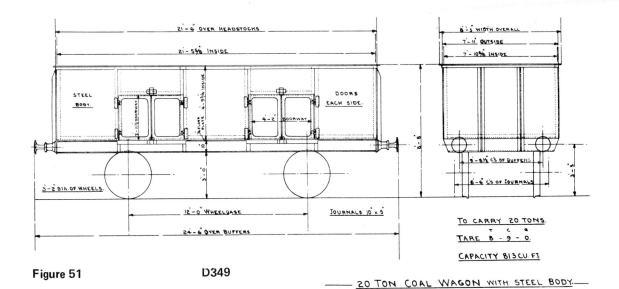

Figure 51   D349

To carry 20 tons.
Tare 8 - 9 - 0.
Capacity 813 cu. ft.

20 TON COAL WAGON WITH STEEL BODY.

Plate 143

Plate **143** illustrates wagon No. 50622 in original condition.

Photograph British Rail

Plate **144** illustrates D345 in L.M.S. livery. The author does not know the position of the running numbers, they were probably at the left hand end of the vehicle.

Photograph Author's Collection

Plate **145** illustrates the alternative method of brake gear on these vehicles. As can be seen on **Plate No. 143**, the brakes were applied by turning a wheel, whereas, on this picture, a brake lever was applied. It is not known how many were so equipped.

Photograph British Rail

Plate 144   Plate 145

Plate 146

Plates 146 and 147 These two pictures depict the original condition of the wooden bodied vehicles and in L.M.S. ownership. It is probable that L.M.S. was painted where the M.R. is located but the position of LOCO COAL is open to conjecture.

Photographs British Rail

Known Running Numbers

D345	2837
D346	12510
D349	35259,
	50622
D350	34993

Plate 147

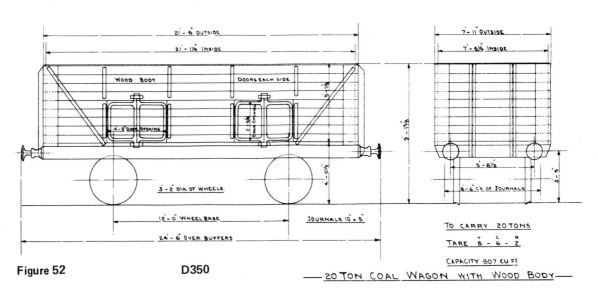

Figure 52   **D350**

TO CARRY 20 TONS
TARE 8 - 6 - 2
CAPACITY 807 CU FT

— 20 TON COAL WAGON WITH WOOD BODY —

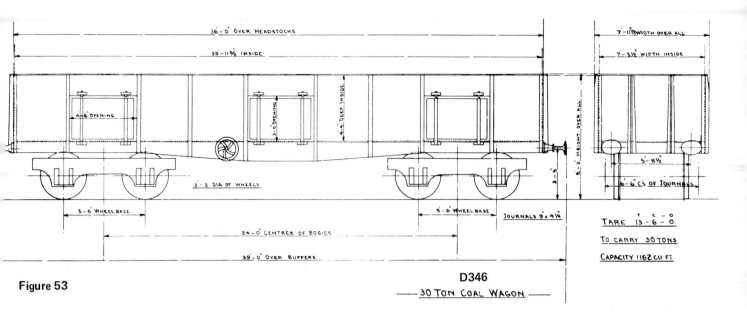

Figure 53

D346

— 30 TON COAL WAGON —

30 TON BOGIE COAL WAGONS

There is no written evidence in the lot book regarding these vehicles and the author is unable to give as complete a story as would be desirable, nevertheless, what is known is recorded below.

The Midland Railway issued three diagrams:— D346—Fig. No. 53, D347—Fig. No. 54, D348—Fig. No. 55 and they were referred to as Leeds Forge, American, and Birmingham. As will be seen the chief difference was in the bogie design. The Leeds Forge built 30 wagons in 1902 and they were described in the 'Locomotive' in November of that year.

The only picture of a train of 30 ton vehicles known to the author.

Photograph British Rail

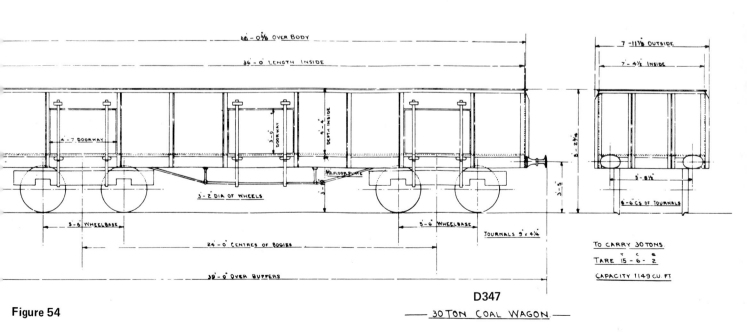

Figure 54

D347

— 30 TON COAL WAGON. —

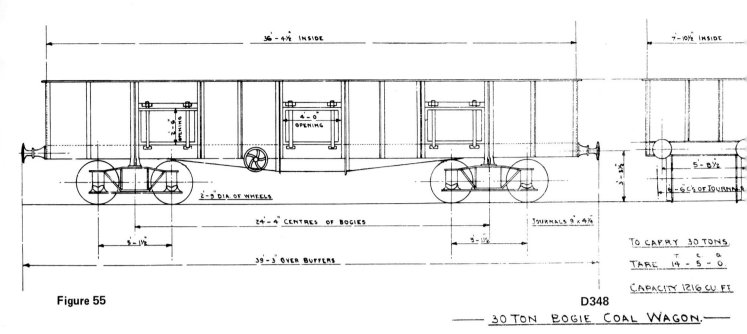

36' - 4½" INSIDE   7' - 10½" INSIDE

2' - 6" OPENING

4' - 0" OPENING

2' - 9" DIA OF WHEELS

24' - 4" CENTRES OF BOGIES

JOURNALS 9 × 4¾

5' - 1½"

5' - 1½"

39' - 3" OVER BUFFERS

3' - 8½"

5' - 8½"

6' - 6 C's OF JOURNALS

Figure 55

D348

TO CARRY 30 TONS.

TARE   T   C   Q
      14 - 5 - 0.

CAPACITY 1216 CU FT

— 30 TON BOGIE COAL WAGON. —

Plate No. 148 illustrates Leeds Forge built wagon No. 12510 which is the only number known to the author. Examples of other bogie vehicles appear in background views but the bogie details cannot be determined. It is quite possible that there were only single examples of the other two diagrams and that only vehicles to D346 existed in quantity. See picture on page 101.

Plate

Chapter 4   Open Wagons for Special Traffic

This term 'open wagons for special traffic' has been selected to encompass all the wagons which were not classified as goods and/or mineral or which appear in the 'Special Wagon' chapters. The types described are as below:—

Long Low-sided Wagons Diagrams 336 & 336a Figs. 56 & 57

The only difference between these two diagrams was in the journal size, 8" x 3½" for the 8-ton capacity wagon and 9" x 3¾" for the 10 ton capacity vehicle which gave codes of LLF and LLH respectively.

Drawing No.	Lot	Qty.	Date	
1062	354	100	1895	D336
	446	100	1898	
	470	100	1899	
	748	200	1910	
Total		500		

The lot book describes these wagons as 'long low-sided wagons for agricultural implements.' The development of the design can be seen in **Plates 149—152.**

Examples were still running until early 1950's.

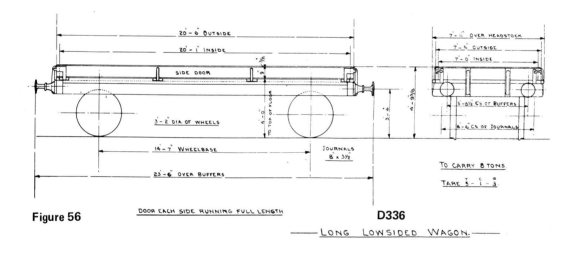

Figure 56   DOOR EACH SIDE RUNNING FULL LENGTH   **D336**

—— LONG LOWSIDED WAGON. ——

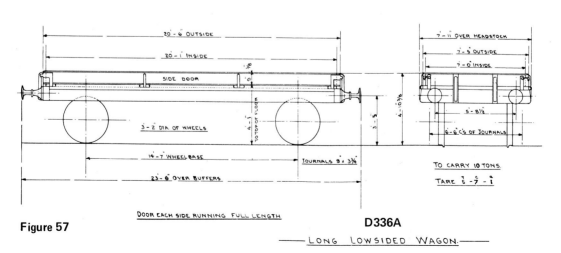

Figure 57   DOOR EACH SIDE RUNNING FULL LENGTH   **D336A**

—— LONG LOWSIDED WAGON. ——

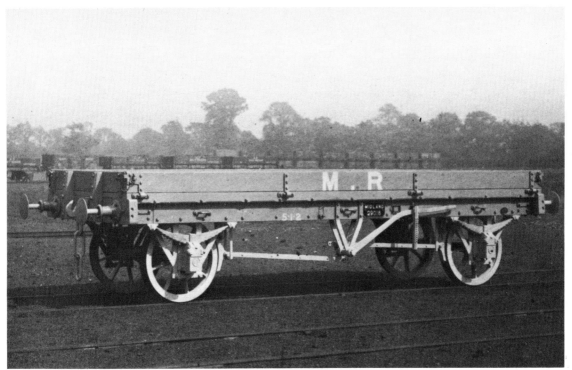

Plate 149

Plate 149 This illustrates wagon No. 29018 in 'as built' condition and is from lot 354 showing the 1895 livery. Note one side brake, compare with **Plate 150**.

Plate 150 Loading a Rolls Royce chassis at Derby on wagon No. 26047 during the early years of this century. Apart from showing the 'No Brake Side' it also illustrates Midland livery in the 20th century.

Both Photographs British Rail

Plate 150

Plate 151 As running in L.M.S. grey livery in 1934. Whereas **Plates 149** and **150** are clearly D336 vehicles it is not clear if this wagon is D336a. Note brakes are now on both sides, axleboxes are oil and marked L.M.S.

Photograph R.E. Lacy

Plate 152 M50782 is a vehicle belonging to D336a. It was photographed in 1952 and its condition is typical of wooden bodied wagons during this period of British Rail ownership. It has been patch painted on the sides and appears to have the smaller 'wartime' size number and 10T with a new M replacing the original L.M.S. which could have preceded the number or have been placed centrally.

Photograph A.E. West

Plate 152

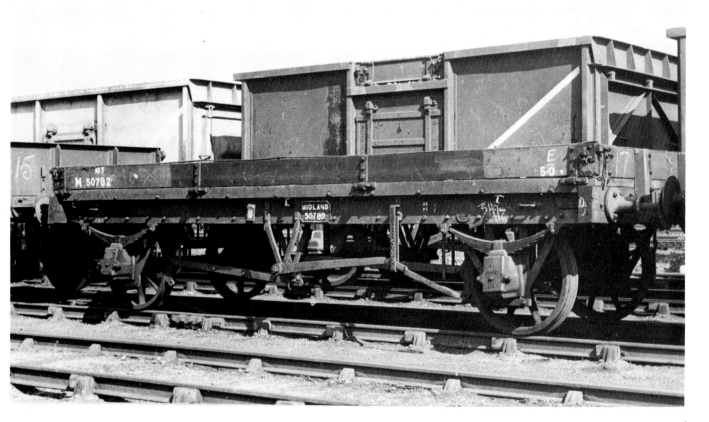

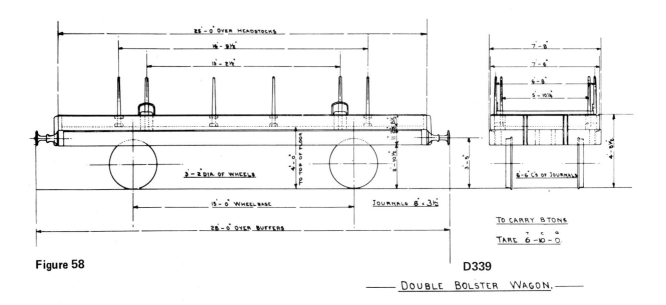

Figure 58

D339

DOUBLE BOLSTER WAGON.

Double Bolster Wagons, Diagrams 339 and 339a

As can be seen from Figs. 58 & 59 the only difference between the two diagrams 339 and 339a, is the position and location of the bolsters. In D339a the bolsters are fixed at 15' 0" apart and in D339 they are 13' 2½" apart but with what appears to be optional uprights, located inside the side sheeting. The constructional details are as below:—

Drawing No.	Lot	Qty.	Date
1113	383	100	1896
	442	200	1898
Total		300	

The lot book suggests that lots 383 and 442 were identical and lot 629 was similar, but it was also described as a 'girder wagon' (see **Plate 286**, Volume II). It is not known how many wagons were built to each diagram. Possibly lot 383 was to D339 and lot 442 to D339a, but this is by no means certain; see **Plates 153—156**. Examples were still running until c1950.

Plate 153 illustrates an example of lo 383, wagon No. 27794.

Photograph British Rai

Plate 154

Plate 154 shows a heavy load on wagon No. 34683 and No. 2686? The brake-work appears to be in the same colour as the body, which is somewhat puzzling, since they are not in photographic livery.
Photograph British Rail

Plate 155 No. 32716 in final L.M.S. livery style of bauxite body colour and black underwork. By now, this vehicle has both side brakes, but still retains its original Midland axleboxes and displays the non common user mark 'N' at each end.
Photographed in May 1939 A. E. West

Plate 156 This has been included to illustrate the inside view of one of these wagons. Regrettably, its number is not known. The date is the early years of this century and the location is Lawley Street, Birmingham.

Photograph British Rail

— DOUBLE BOLSTER WAGON. —

25'-0" OVER HEADSTOCKS
15'-0"
4'-0" TO TOP OF FLOOR
3'-2" DIA OF WHEELS
15'-0" WHEEL BASE
JOURNALS 8" x 3½
28'-0" OVER BUFFERS

7'-8"
7'-6"
5'-10½"
6'-6 C'S OF JOURNALS

D339A
TO CARRY 8 TONS
TARE 6-9-2

Figure 59

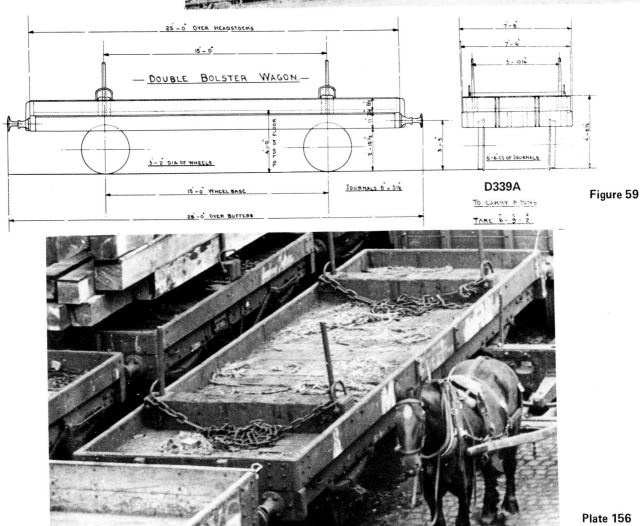

Plate 156

107

Plate 157

TO CARRY 1½ TONS IN EACH BOX
TARE 6 - 1 - 0. (OF WAGON)
CAPACITY OF EACH BOX 66 CU. FT

Plate 157 Midland bunker coal wagons in L.M.S. ownership. The legend, 'L.M.S. Steamer Coal,' can just be seen where 'Empty to Embsay' is located on **Plate 158**, and both pictures clearly show the non common user markings. It is presumed that all the vehicle was painted grey, apart from the normal, 'below the solebar black', ruling.

Photograph British Rail

Plate 158 A board stating 'Empty to Embsay' covers the 'L.M.S. Steamer Coal' legend and it is presumed that this change of use followed the change from coal to oil for the steamers, whose fuel was originally carried in these containers. Alternative work was then found for these wagons, as illustrated in this picture.

Photograph British Rail

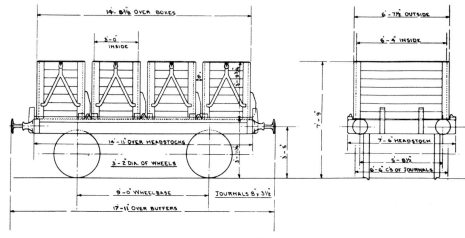

FOR THE CONVEYANCE OF BUNKER COAL TO HEYSHAM.

——— LOCO. BUNKER COAL WAGON ———

Loco Bunker Coal Wagon D721 Figure 60

The lot book contains no record for this type of vehicle. Loco bunker coal wagons existed in considerable numbers and **Fig. 60** illustrates their dimensions. Almost certainly they were produced by using existing 14' 11" chassis, probably from D299 high goods, which were cut down to floor level, and the bunker built new—the probable date of construction being 1904 (when Heysham was opened). Photographs exist, showing a complete train and the livery in Midland days was 'M.R. Steamer Coal' along the side and **Plate 157** shows the same vehicles in L.M.S. days, with 'L.M.S.' replacing the 'M.R.' They lasted in steamer coal traffic until the 1930's when the ships converted to oil and then they were used for stone traffic ex Embsay or Rylstone. Little else is known about this type, and they are illustrated in **Plates 157—158**. Dates of withdrawal are not known.

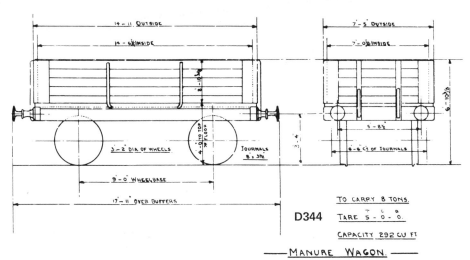

D344

TO CARRY 8 TONS.
TARE 5 - 0 - 0.
CAPACITY 292 CU FT

—— MANURE WAGON. ——

Manure Wagon—Diagram 344 Figure 61

To all intents, this wagon is D299, without side doors and the lot book records the following information:—

Drawing No.	Lot	Qty.	Date	
550A	334	20	1894	Fitted with splash boards at ends.
	350	20	1895	Without splash boards
	411	32	1897	Without splash boards
	436	30	1898	Without splash boards
Total		102		

The only known photograph appears in **Plate 159**. Date of withdrawal not known.

Plate 159 The only known photograph of a manure wagon is No. 76417. The sole-bar plate reads 'To be returned to Nottingham when empty'. It is presumed that some lasted to carry early L.M.S. livery similar to that carried by the high goods version and that the manure traffic was generated by cattle in transit. However very little is known by the author regarding this particular aspect of railway working.

Photograph British Rail

Plate 159

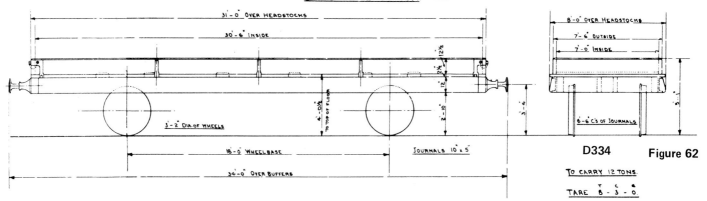

LONG RAIL WAGON.

31'-0" OVER HEADSTOCKS
30'-6" INSIDE
3'-2" DIA OF WHEELS
18'-0" WHEELBASE
34'-0" OVER BUFFERS
JOURNALS 10" x 5"
4'-0" TO TOP OF FLOOR

8'-0" OVER HEADSTOCKS
7'-6" OUTSIDE
7'-0" INSIDE
6'-6" C's OF JOURNALS

D334   Figure 62

TO CARRY 12 TONS
TARE 8-3-0

Long Rail Wagon Diagram 334 Figure 62

These wagons, 30' 6'' long inside, were branded 'Stores Dept,' and generally used for departmental work. However, the vehicle illustrated in **Plate 161** suggests this may not have always been the case. Note cross planks shown on the diagram, on the floor of the vehicle to raise the load and leave space for lifting chains. Unlike the short rail wagons which had fixed sides, these vehicles had full length drop sides.

The lot book information records:—

Drawing No.	Lot	Qty.	Date	
871	299	50	1892	
	353	50	1895	
	377	50	1896	
	465	180	1899	(30 were recorded as renewals)
Total		330		

Plate 160

Plates 160/161 These two plates illustrate a wagon in original condition and as running some 25—30 years later. Wagon No. 19310 (**Plate 160**) is an example of lot 299 in its 1893 livery while wagon No. 117063 (**Plate 161**) shows how the vehicle ran in early L.M.S. ownership—still with the brake only on one side, even though it now has oil axleboxes.

Both Photographs British Rail

Two illustrations of these wagons appear in Plates 160/161.

110

Plate 161

Short Rail Wagon Diagram 335 and 335a Figures 63 & 64

The lot book records the following information

Drawing No.	Lot	Qty.	Date	
811	238	65	1889	12 ton D335
	722	6	1909	15 ton D335a
Total		71		

Examples of both long and short rail wagons were in existence until c1950.

The 15 ton vehicles were slightly higher as noted on the diagram. **Plates 162–164** record these wagons.

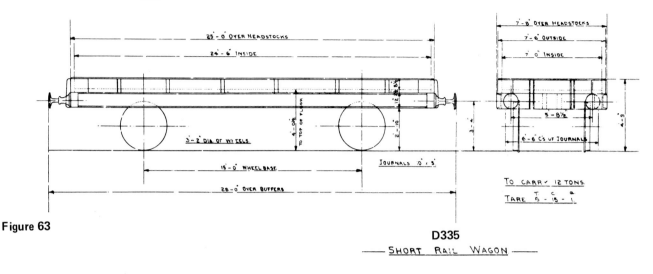

Figure 63

D335

—— SHORT RAIL WAGON ——

Plates 162–164 all illustrate the short rail wagon in varying conditions. **Plate 162** is an 1890 picture of wagon No. 39476 and it is interesting to note that the short vehicles didn't rate the legend, 'Dept.'— see **Plate 160**.

Photograph British Rail

Plate 162

Figure 64   D335A   —— SHORT RAIL WAGON ——

Plate 163

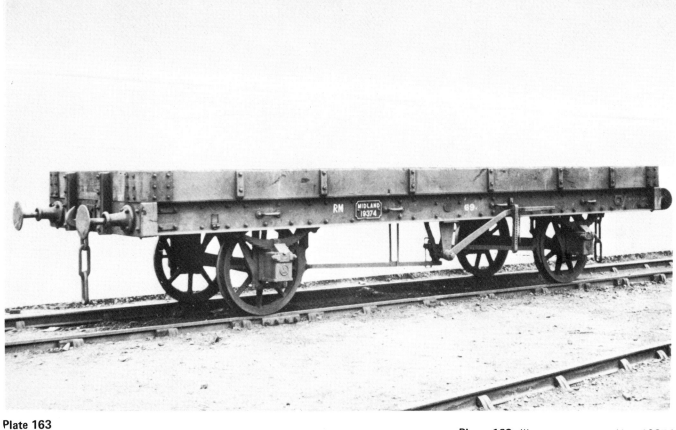

Plate 163

Plate 163 illustrates wagon No. 19374 and the white background to this official picture shows up the details. Both plates 162 and 163 are to D335.

Photograph British Rail

Plate 164

Plate 164 illustrates wagon No. 23214 of diagram 335a photographed in 1946 in L.M.S. grey livery with the wartime numbering in the post-1936 position, usually associated with vehicles in bauxite livery. Note oil axleboxes, it now has an L.M.S. numberplate in place of its original Midland plate and it will have brakes on both sides of the vehicle.

Photograph A.G. Ellis

112

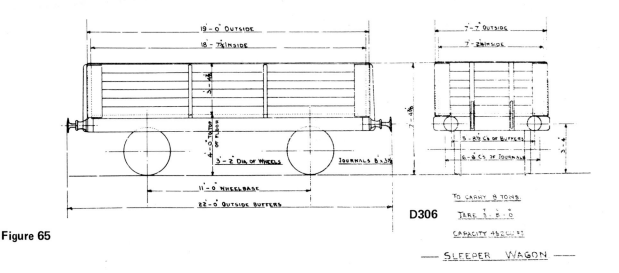

Figure 65

D306

TO CARRY 8 TONS.
TARE 5 - 8 - 0
CAPACITY 452 CU FT

— SLEEPER WAGON —

Sleeper Wagons Diagrams 306 and 307 Figures 65 & 66

Two diagrams were issued for the same size vehicle, D306 having fixed sides, D307 was so constructed to allow the top three planks to fold down, thus making the loading and unloading of sleepers somewhat easier. The lot book records the following:—

Drawing No.	Lot	Qty.	Date	
535	70	50	1881	
	137	20	1885	
	273	175	1891	According to plate 14. This was the second style—but drawing no. not changed.
1456	495	50	1900	Similar to lot 273 on standard underframe
Total		295		

It appears that drawing 535 refers to D306 and drawing 1456 to D307. However, some of D307 were built to D306 drawing! (see **Plates 165 and 166**). Livery in L.M.S. days could have been red oxide as with other engineers stock but this is not known for certain. It is possible that examples remained in service until c1950.

Plates 165 and 166 *(overleaf)* These are the only known pictures of these vehicles with visible numbers and clearly illustrate the 1881 and 1892 livery styles. It is presumed that post-1900, D306 would have been liveried as D307 wagon No. 4887. Just what livery was carried post-1923 (as and when repainted by the L.M.S.) is not known—possibly grey with 'L.M.S.' replacing 'M.R.' being the only alteration.

Both Photographs British Rail

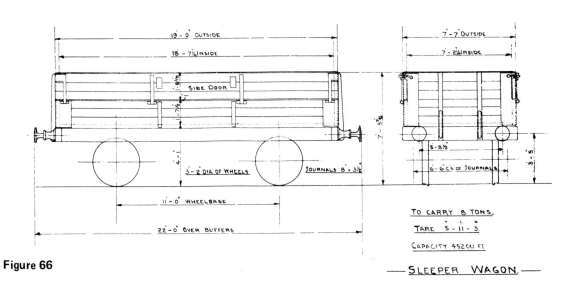

Figure 66

TO CARRY 8 TONS.
TARE 5 - 11 - 3.
CAPACITY 452 CU FT

— SLEEPER WAGON. —

Plate 165

Plate 166

Timber Trucks—Short—Diagram 388 Figure 67

Timber trucks date from the early days of railways and were the smallest Midland wagons to feature in the diagram book. Although it has been recorded that the Midland was using spring buffers for all new wagon stock from 1855 this is not true for timber trucks which were built well after this date, with dumb buffers. Exactly when the Midland began to fit spring buffers to its short timber trucks and how many of those which were originally built with dumb buffers but later fitted with spring buffers is not known. One drawing only was used for all the short timber trucks built from 1878 and the drawing number suggests that lot 14 was the first batch to have been built using this particular drawing. Reference to the plates will summarise the position as known and the lot book records in the next column, the following:—

Scrapping of the dumb buffered stock would have been completed before the outbreak of World War 1 and those with spring buffers would have lasted until c1940.

The reference in the lot book to old and new brakes is further discussed in the captions to **Plates 167** and **168**.

Drawing No.	Lot	Qty.	Date	
366	14	200	1878	
	44	100	1880	
	62	300	1881	70 Old Brake—230 New
	90	100	1883	
	107	100	1884	
	129	200	1885	
	156	200	1886	
	184	200	1887	
	222	250	1889	
	254	100	1890	
	294	50	1892	
	330	14	1893	
	362	50	1895	
Total		1864		

Figure 67

Plate 167

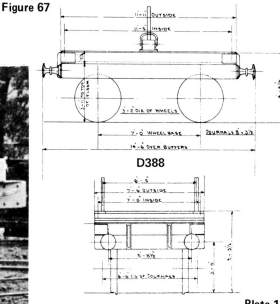

D388

This illustration of a dumb buffered short timber truck represents an example of lot 101. **Plate No. 167** shows vehicle No. 18080 with new brakes!

Plate 168

Plate 168 which illustrates Gloucester C. & W. Co. Ltd. vehicle No. 12206, is an example of earlier construction and, apart from the early livery referred to in Chapter 2, attention is drawn to a number of detail differences of axlebox, vee hanger, brake, and wheel arrangements. Note also the 3 link couplings and safety chains.

Photographs: Plate No. 167 British Rail
Plate No. 168 Author's Collection

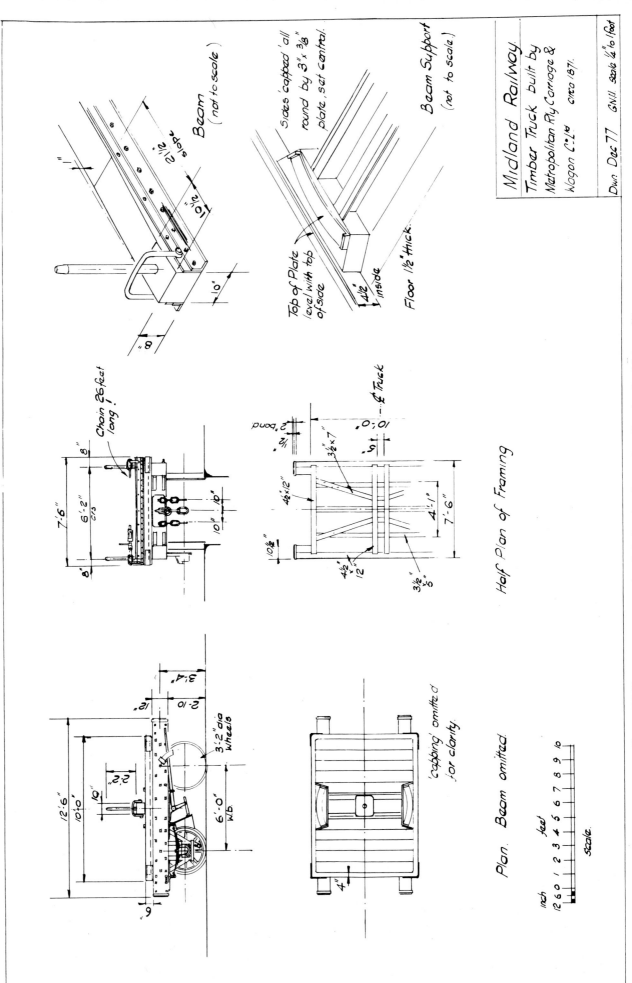

Figure 68 illustrates an example of timber truck construction by the Metropolitan Railway Carriage & Wagon Company Ltd., c1871, and is similar to truck No. 12206,

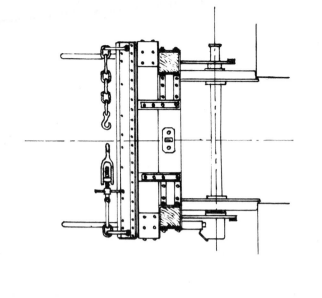

MIDLAND RLY. LONG TIMBER TRUCK
M.R. DRG No. 399 LOT 77

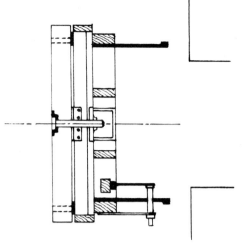

Figure 69 illustrates lot No. // as featured in **Plate No. 169**.
Some of these trucks were later rebuilt with spring buffers and examples of these vehicles will be found in **Plate No. 171**.

Drawing K. C. Woodhead

0 1 2 3 4 5 6 7 8 Ft.

17

Timber Trucks—Long, Diagram 389 Fig. 70

One diagram only covers all the long timber trucks built by the Midland even though the earliest examples were apparently built with dumb buffers (see Fig. 69.) The lot book records the following information.

Drawing No.	Lot	Qty.	Date
559	77	200	1882
	505	540	1901
2970	698	100	1908
	704	50	1908
3383	742	100	1910
	770	200	1911
	787	200	1911
	895	100	1915
Total		1490	

Probably all of lot 77 were built with dumb buffers as Fig. 69 but in due course some of them were equipped with spring buffers. A number of vehicles were still running in the early 1950's. **Plates 169—173** illustrate various examples of this type of vehicle.

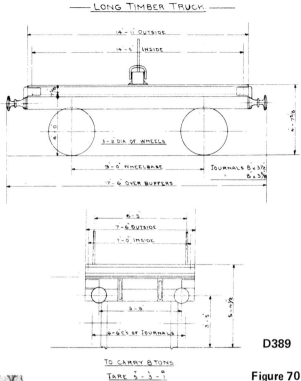

LONG TIMBER TRUCK

D389

Figure 70

Plate 169 The picture of truck No. 34709 illustrates an example of a long timber truck built to lot 77 (see Fig. 69) and should be compared with **Plates 170—173** which illustrate later examples of these vehicles.

Photograph British Rail

Plates 170—173 illustrate various examples of D336 and the sequence is designed to show the livery development rather than building sequence. Assuming that truck 17951, (**Plate 170**) is not carrying a replacement numberplate then it is probably an example of lot 895 built to drawing 3383. Note the shallower sides as compared with truck No. 34709, **Plate 169**.

Photograph Author's Collection

Plate 170

Plate 171 Reading from left to right the trucks are Midland Nos. 7206, 144896, 33?34, centre number unidentified and "unknown number." The trucks display two heights of side and only 7206, with the shallower side carries the final style of number plate which seems to suggest that 144896, 33?34 and "unknown number" are to drawing 2970 or 559. The centre two trucks have grease axleboxes, the outer two oil which, in the author's opinion, confirms 7206 as being lot 895, "unknown number" lot 698 or 704, and the centre two lot 505 or lot 77 with spring buffers. So much for the origin. Note how the load has been secured. It runs on the first and third truck, the second has the bolster removed, this vehicle plus the right hand truck being runners. The question is, where was the replaced bolster placed? This picture is part of a timber train. Was there an open wagon in the train to carry the displaced bolsters? The author freely admits lack of information on this point.

Finally, attention is drawn to the 'dumb buffer' rebuilds. The two centre vehicles in **Plate 171** were originally built with dumb buffers, but have had them removed and replaced by self-contained spring buffers. However, the headstock does not extend the full width of the wagon.

Photograph British Rail

Plate 173

Plate 172 Timber trucks were common user, as shown in this illustration of Midland truck No. 18183, in company with G.W.R. trucks Nos. 70287/8. The picture has been selected to illustrate this aspect and to show the lettering position during the first L.M.S. livery period.

Photograph British Rail

Plate 173 Truck No. 11114 near the end of its life in September 1947. It is impossible to say if it is bauxite or grey. The lettering style is 'Wartime'. The position and style represents the post-1936 position.

Photograph Author's Collection

Plate 174 This is a total mystery. T
original print, now in the author's coll
tion, came from the late W. O. Steel a
was marked 'M.R. Sleeper Wagon—Ap
1946'. There is no reference in the
book or diagram book to anything of t
nature. However, in 1926, the L.M
managed to build two chaired slee
trolleys at Derby, without either a d
gram or lot number, so perhaps the L.M
merely followed the Midland's examp
See page 101, *The L.M.S. Wagon*, Dav
& Charles, 1977.

Photograph A.G. E

Running Numbers ⊕ one sided brake.

D336 and D336a Long Low-sided

26042 Tare 4.19.0 ⊕	50782 Tare 5.0
76476 Tare —	83428 Tare 5.6
29018 — 5.1.2 ⊕	75895 Tare 5.11
78693 Tare —	

D339 and D339a Double Bolster Wagons

2822 Tare 6.9.0 ⊕	26786 Tare — ⊕
27794 Tare 5.6.0 ⊕	32716 Tare 6.0

D721 Loco Bunker Coal

None known

D344 Manure Wagon

76417 Tare 5.0.0 ⊕

D334 Long Rail Wagon

116898 Tare — ⊕	117063 Tare 7.12.0
19310 Tare 8.3.0	

D335 and D335a Short Rail Wagons

19374 Tare 6.9 ⊕	39476 Tare 6.15.1 ⊕
39497 Tare 6.16.0 ⊕	15 ton 23214 Tare —

D306 Sleeper Wagon   D307

33789 ⊕ Tare —	4887 Tare 5.10.2 ⊕
	111691 Tare —

D388 Short Timber Truck Dumb Buffers

12206 Tare 4.11.0 ⊕	18080 Tare 4.12.3 ⊕

D389 Long Timber Trucks

Dumb Buffer 34709 Tare 4.19.1
Spring Buffer 1124 Tare — ⊕

1336 Tare — ⊕	7206 Tare 5.1.0 ⊕
8592 Tare — ⊕	11114 Tare 4.12
144896 Tare 5.2.0 ⊕	17945 Tare — ⊕
17951 Tare 5.3.0	18025 Tare — ⊕
18083 Tare 5.0	18183 Tare 5.6.0
23718 Tare — ⊕	27109 Tare 4.19
32687 Tare 5.3.1	34709 Tare 4.19.1

Some evidence of runs are suggested by the above e.g. 1124—1336, 17945—51, 18025—18183. However the possibility of other types being within the possible 'run' cannot be overlooked.

Bristol St. Philip's on 30th May 1922.

Photograph British Rail, courtesy National Railway Museu

Chapter 5 Covered Goods Wagons

The early development of covered goods wagons was considered in chapter one, and this chapter will only consider vehicles built during the period 1880—1923, and will deal with vehicles rated for goods or goods and fruit traffic and tariff vans—all other covered vans being discussed in chapter six.

Midland goods van construction, which the Midland generally called covered goods wagons, can be broken down into three distinct groups, i.e. 14' 11'' over headstocks with a 9' 0'' wheelbase; 16' 6'' over headstocks with a 10' 0'' wheelbase and 17' 6'' over headstocks with a 10' 0'' wheelbase. At this juncture, it must be admitted that not all the questions posed have been answered to the author's complete satisfaction, but it is believed that the following sequence is correct:—

The earliest drawing issued for covered goods wagon construction after the opening of the new works, was for drawing No. 401, and construction covered the period 1880—1892 although, by that date, Derby were apparently building vans 6'' and 12'' higher than previous lots, to the same drawing number! During this period, two covered goods wagons were built to drawing No. 750 in 1888, and they are illustrated in Chapter 6 (Fig. No. 106). Apart from these two vehicles, construction was all to the basic design and the details are below:—

14' 11'' Over Headstocks

Covered Goods Wagons built to Drawing 401

Figures 71—79.

Diagram No.	Lot	Qty.	Date	
D353	48	50	1880	
D353	116	210	1884	
D353	136	20	1885	
D353	157	100	1886	
D353	182	170	1887	
D375	182	30	1887	With Vents
D353	209	320	1888	
D375	209	30	1888	With Vents
D353	236	100	1889	
D353	248	150	1890	
D353	287	100	1891	
D356	309	50	1892	6'' higher than previous lots
D357 ⎫ D358 ⎬ D359 ⎭	309	164	1892	12'' higher than previous lots
D376	309	6	1892	12'' higher than previous lots with brake pipe
Total		1500		

Examination of Fig. drawings 71, 73—75, 77—79 reveals that, of the 1,500 vehicles constructed, 1,220 were built to D353 (Figs. 71 and 72) and 60 were built to D375 (Fig. 73)

which was a ventilated version of the basic covered vehicle, and these 60 built to D375 were classified as fruit vans. Before leaving this small vehicle, attention should be drawn to the brake variations, as noted on the diagrams. Regrettably, no information exists as to the quantities of each type or any running numbers, other than vehicles illustrated in **Plates 175** and **176**.

Fig. 74 covered the 50 vehicles built to lot 309, with an extra 6'' plank which increased D353 from 9' 11³⁄₈'' from rail to roof top to 10' 5³⁄₈'' from rail to roof top and these vehicles were classified D356.

Lot 309, which comprised 220 vehicles, holds the record for different diagram numbers. After allocating 50, which were 6'' higher than previous lots, the final 170 were divided between four other diagrams and, apart from the six allocated to D376, it is not known just how many of the remaining 164 vans were built to D357/358/359, Figs. 75, 77, 78. Nevertheless, the details as indicated on the diagrams are as follows:—

D357	13'' higher, some fitted with AVB through pipes	
D358	12'' higher, plus height of hatchway on roof, which lifts off. Apparently all handbrake only.	
D359	13'' higher, plus height of sliding roof, which opened up an area on one side only. Apparently all handbrake only.	
D376	12'' higher, with vents, rated as fruit vans, fitted with AVB through pipe.	

It would appear that the Midland was experimenting with roof doors and, since no further vehicles were so constructed it must be concluded that the experiment was not a complete success.

The life of these early vehicles was probably until c1935 but further construction to D357 was made during 1903—06. The lot book records:—

Drawing No.	Lot	Qty.	Date	
1830	562	2,496	1903	8-ton to use existing material
	625	471	1905	
Total		2,967		

As will be noted, this construction was preceded by longer 16' 6'' vans, and one wonders just how or what 8-ton material was on hand. It is possible that it refers to material which was ordered for D299 high goods wagons, whose construction ceased in 1901/2, with the exception of 10 built in 1906 and 1,000 in 1917, which also may have been to use up material ordered for low goods wagons and referred to in chapter 1, page 25. However, whatever the exact circumstances were, almost 3,000 more 8-ton covered goods wagons to D357 were placed in service. Fig 76 is a drawing based upon Derby works drawing No. 1830 which, in effect, was what Derby had built ten years earlier to drawing 401! These 4,467 vehicles were all built with single side brake gear and grease axleboxes but, in due course, many received both side brake gear and oil axleboxes—see **Plates 182/183**.

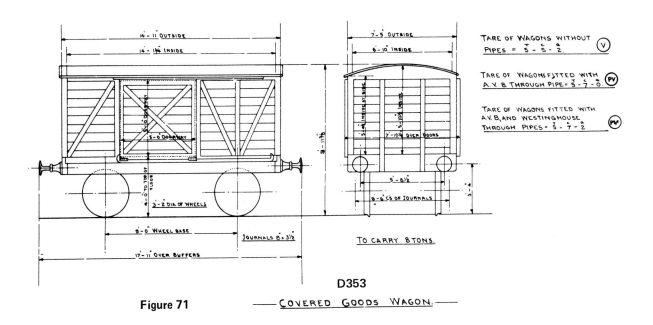

Figure 71

D353

— COVERED GOODS WAGON. —

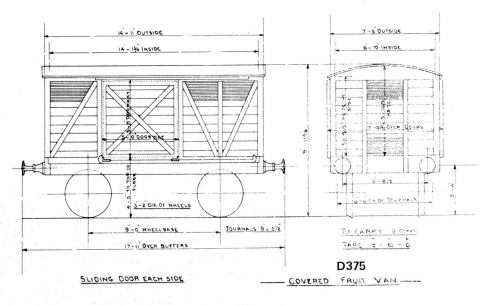

D375

— COVERED FRUIT VAN. —

SLIDING DOOR EACH SIDE

Figure 72
This drawing, produced from general arrangement drawing No. 401, depicts D353 in original condition.

Drawing G.K. Fox

Figure 73

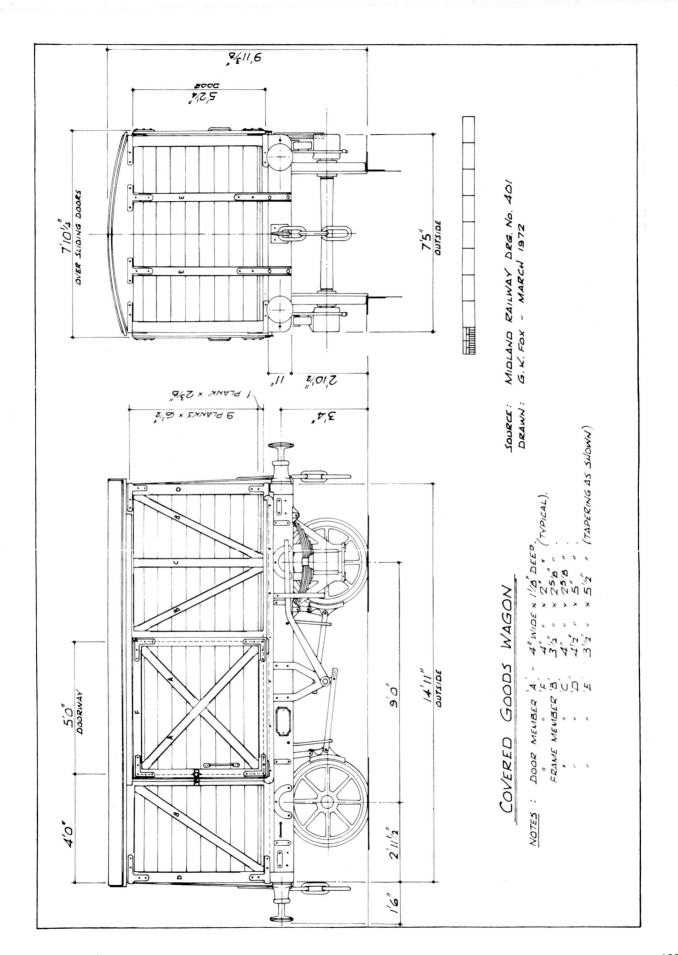

COVERED GOODS WAGON

SOURCE: MIDLAND RAILWAY DRG. No. 401
DRAWN: G.K. FOX – MARCH 1972

NOTES: DOOR MEMBER 'A' – 4" WIDE x 1½" DEEP (TYPICAL).
" 'F' – 4" " x 2" " "
FRAME MEMBER 'B' – 3½" " x 2⅝" "
" 'C' – 4" " x 2⅝" "
" 'D' – 4½" " x 5" "
" 'E' – 3½" " x 5½" " (TAPERING AS SHOWN)

9'11⅜"

5'2½"
DOOR

7'10½"
OVER SLIDING DOORS

7'5"
OUTSIDE

2'10½"
11"

9 PLANKS x 6½"
1 PLANK x 2⅜"

3'4"

4'0"
5'0"
DOORWAY

9'0"

14'11"
OUTSIDE

2'11½"
1'6"

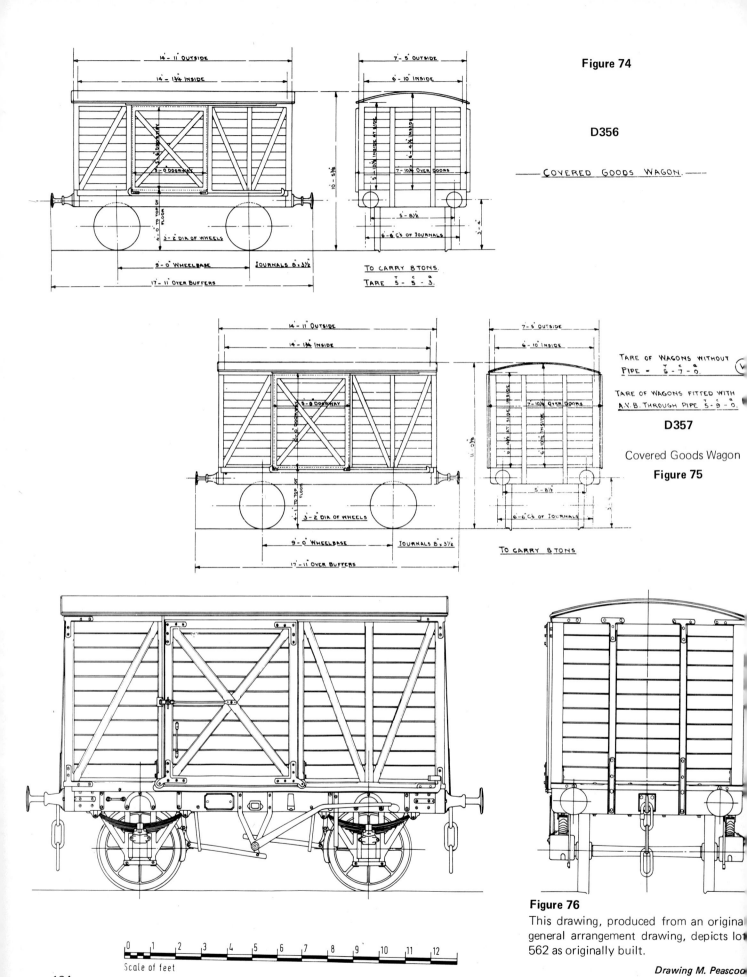

Figure 74

D356

COVERED GOODS WAGON.

14'-11" OUTSIDE
14'-1¾" INSIDE
7'-5" OUTSIDE
6'-10" INSIDE
10'-5⅜"
5'-0 DOORWAY
7'-10½" OVER DOORS
3'-2 DIA OF WHEELS
9'-0" WHEELBASE
JOURNALS 8"x3½"
17'-11" OVER BUFFERS
6'-6" C's OF JOURNALS
5'-8½"
3'-4"

TO CARRY 8 TONS.
TARE 5-5-3.

Figure 75

D357

Covered Goods Wagon

14'-11" OUTSIDE
14'-1¾" INSIDE
7'-5" OUTSIDE
6'-10" INSIDE
5'-0 DOORWAY
7'-10½" OVER DOORS
3'-2 DIA OF WHEELS
9'-0" WHEELBASE
JOURNALS 8"x3½"
17'-11" OVER BUFFERS
6'-6" C's OF JOURNALS
5'-8½"

TO CARRY 8 TONS

TARE OF WAGONS WITHOUT
PIPE = 5-7-0.

TARE OF WAGONS FITTED WITH
A.V.B. THROUGH PIPE 5-9-0.

Figure 76

This drawing, produced from an original
general arrangement drawing, depicts lot
562 as originally built.

Drawing M. Peascod

Scale of feet
0 1 2 3 4 5 6 7 8 9 10 11 12

124

Figure 77

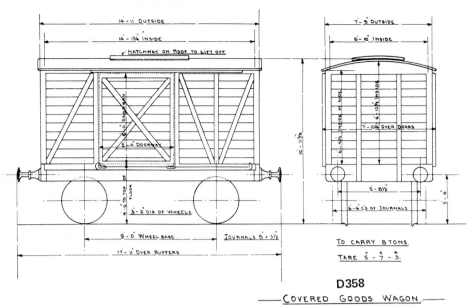

14'-11" OUTSIDE
14'-1¾" INSIDE
HATCHWAY ON ROOF TO LIFT OFF.
7'-5" OUTSIDE
6'-10" INSIDE

6'-0" DOORWAY
5'-0" DOORWAY
7'-10¾" OVER DOORS

10'-11⅜"

9'-0" TO TOP OF FLOOR
3'-2 DIA OF WHEELS

5'-8½"
6'-6 C'S OF JOURNALS
3'-4

9'-0" WHEEL BASE
JOURNALS 8" x 3½"
17'-11" OVER BUFFERS

TO CARRY 8 TONS.
TARE 5 - 7 - 3.

D358

—— COVERED GOODS WAGON. ——

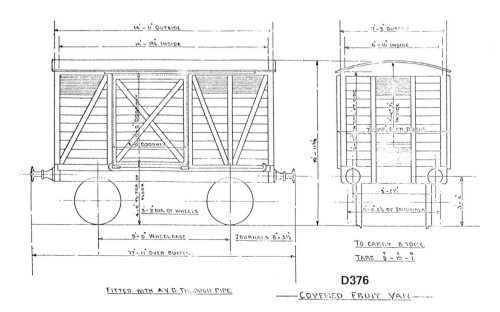

14'-11" OUTSIDE
14'-1¾" INSIDE
4'-0" OPENING IN ROOF
7'-5" OUTSIDE
6'-10" INSIDE
SLIDING ROOF

5'-0" DOORWAY
7'-10¾" OVER DOORS

11'-0⅜"

6'-10½" INSIDE

9'-0" TO TOP OF FLOOR
3'-2 DIA OF WHEELS

5'-8½"
6'-6 C'S OF JOURNALS
3'-5

9'-0" WHEELBASE
JOURNALS 8" x 3½"
17'-11" OVER BUFFERS

TO CARRY 8 TONS.
TARE 5 - 12 - 0.

Figure 78

D359

—— COVERED GOODS WAGON. ——

14'-11" OUTSIDE
14'-1¾" INSIDE
7'-5" OUTSIDE
6'-10" INSIDE

DOORWAY
DOORWAY
7'-10¾" OVER DOORS

10'-11⅜"

TOP OF FLOOR
3'-2 DIA OF WHEELS

5'-8½"
6'-6 C'S OF JOURNALS
3'-4

9'-0" WHEELBASE
JOURNALS 8" x 3½"
17'-11" OVER BUFFERS

TO CARRY 8 TONS.
TARE 5 - 15 - 1.

D376

—— COVERED FRUIT VAN. ——

Figure 79

FITTED WITH A.V.B. THROUGH PIPE.

125

Plate 175 illustrates covered fruit van No. 30069 of D375, which is believed to be from lot 182 and is the only picture of this type known to the author. Comparison with the diagram suggests that perhaps the diagram is in error with regard to the depth of the ventilators. Unlike the majority of covered vehicles, which the Midland referred to as 'covered wagons', those built to D375 were covered fruit vans and attention is drawn to the A on the door which also appears on D378, see **Plate 198**, also referred to as a 'van'. It is not known what the A signified.

Photo A.G. Ellis Collection

Plate 175

Plate 176

Plates 176 and 177 illustrate two covered goods wagons of D353. **Plate 176** shows van No. 19243 in original condition, with one side brake gear. **Plate 177** is an interesting picture in that the date of the photograph is unknown and unfortunately, the van does not carry a numberplate or painted number on the bodyside. Again, one side only brake gear but, unlike No. 19243, which has solid spoke wheels, this vehicle has open spoke wheels.

Both Photographs British Rail

Plate 177

Plate 178 This is the only known photograph of an example of D356 and illustrates No. 9012 in original condition. Later, this covered goods wagon, together with other vehicles of D353 and D356, would have carried livery similar to that shown in **Plate 180** and, those vehicles which carried L.M.S. livery, would have looked like the vehicle in **Plate 181**. It is most unlikely that many of these early covered goods wagons would have received both side brake gear or oil axle boxes.

Photograph British Rail

Plate 178

Plate 179

Plates 179—183 depict various examples of D357 vehicles in varying conditions.

Plate 179 illustrates No. 114193 in original condition.

Photograph British Rail

Plate 180 shows the livery in Midland days with the number 144438 in the top half of the door. The tare weight would be on the solebar of the left hand end. Apart from the livery, this picture is of interest showing traffic carried and the methods of loading and unloading employed.

Photograph British Rail

Plate 180

Plate 181

Plate **181** illustrates No. 32389, as running c1936. By now, the vehicle has acquired oil axleboxes and both sides brake gear. The livery is L.M.S. grey and, it should be noted, that some vehicles displayed the load above the number (**see Plate 182**).

Photograph G. Y. Hemmingway

Plate **182** illustrates No. 78179 in grey but, when compared with No. 32389, there is no tare weight visible. Dirty grey livery, new oil axleboxes, and both side brake gear.

Photograph Author's Collection

Plate **183** Unfortunately, no pictures are known to exist illustrating the roof door versions. However, this picture of No. 5095, taken in June 1946, displays a rainstrip on the roof; compare with the other pictures which show none at all or full length. As would be expected in 1946, oil axleboxes and, of course, both side brake gear. It is difficult to say if it is painted bauxite or grey—probably the former, with wartime size numbers and L.M.S., all in the correct post-1936 positions. Finally, the addition of angle irons on the end stanchions in L.M.S. days should be noted (**see Plates 182/183**).

Photograph A. G. Ellis

Plate 182

Plate 183

16' 6" COVERED GOODS WAGONS

The 16' 6" over headstock vehicles can be divided into two groups and the batch D360—D364 will be considered first. These five diagrams, Figs. 80—84 are, in effect, a longer version of the earlier 14' 11" vehicles.

The construction details were:—

Diagram	Lot	Qty.	Date	
D362	311	50	1893	Drawing
	329	26	1893	981
Part	342	200	1894	
Total		276		

During the construction of lot 342, a change in the design of the drawgear was made. A new drawing was issued and the construction continued as below to drawing No. 1032.

Diagram No.		Lot	Qty.	Date	
D362		342	100	1894	
		364	10	1895	
		462	450	1899	
D360		462	50	1899	Fitted
D362		503	1,734	1901	
D362	Part	543	500	1902	
Total			2,844		

All of the covered goods wagons built to drawing 1032 were 8-ton capacity and, probably, all were equipped with grease axleboxes with the possible exception of lot 462.

In 1902 a new drawing was issued No. 1642 and this commenced a spate of covered goods wagon building in what can only be described as an unusual pattern of 8-ton and 10-ton capacity, intermixed with other body and brake variations. It is felt that the construction should be recorded in date order, together with the diagram allocations by lot construction.

Diagram No.		Lot	Qty.	Date	
D363	Part	543	1500	1902	
D364	Part	543	350	1902	With louvres & torpedo vents
D364	Part	543	100	1902	Piped, with louvres & torpedo vents
D360	Part	563	150	1903	
D360		585	150	1904	
D363		614	100	1905	
D363		643	150	1906	
D362		658	100	1907	
D362		695	75	1907	

Diagram	Lot	Qty.	Date	
D362	716	50	1909	
D362	721	100	1909	
D362	737	100	1910	
D362	749	50	1910	
D363	824	100	1913	Also drg. 3190
D363	832	100	1913	Also drg. 3190
D363	863	100	1913	Also drg. 3190
D363	866	300	1914	
D363	900	300	1915	Also drg. 3190
D362	914	200	1916	
Total		4,075		

The reference to drawing 3190 is confusing, and it is not clear just what this covered. The author believes that it marked the beginning of both side brake gear, but this is not confirmed.

In addition to the foregoing vehicles, further construction to this batch brought the total number of vehicles up to 7261. The additional vehicles were as below:—

Drawing No. 1822

Diagram No.		Lot	Qty.	Date	
D361	Part	563	50	1903	5-ton fitted
D364		723	16	1909	Fruit

It should be noted, however, that there were considerable variations within this group of vehicles and **Plates 184 to 196** cover livery and construction styles. Examples of these vehicles remained in service for many years—the ventilated varieties being scrapped first and, almost certainly, not surviving the Second World War, but the basic covered goods wagons lasted until the late 1950's, with some examples preserved today at Butterley.

Before moving on to consider the other 16' 6" long vehicles with different door arrangements, there is one batch of covered goods wagons which are, in effect, D363 as far as overall dimensions are concerned. The lot book contains the following information:—

Drawing No.	Lot	Qty.	Date	
4427	938	100		10-ton
	941	100		
Total		200		

The most likely explanation is that they were to use up material on hand, possibly ordered for 'overseas' construction and, for some reason, the side bracing was altered. No diagram was issued, the basic measurements being identical to D363 (see **Plates 194—196**).

Plate 1

Diagrams 362 and 363 are considered together in **Plates 184** and **187—196. Plate 184** illustrates No. 114351 with its 21.8.1893 paint date clearly visible on the solebar. This is one of the original batch of 50 built to lot 311. Later, the grease axleboxes would be replaced by oil with both sides brakegear fitted. Shortly after this photograph was taken covered goods wagons began to be lettered "M.R." and the position was on the door. See **Plate 180.**

Photograph British Rail

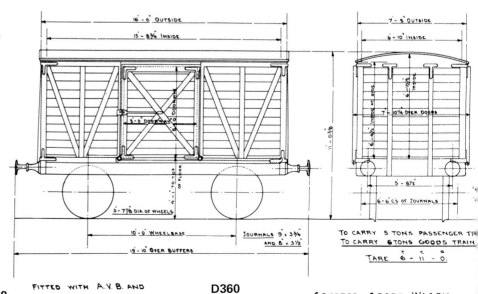

Figure 80 FITTED WITH A.V.B. AND HAND BRAKE COMPLETE. D360 —— COVERED GOODS WAGON. ——

Figure 81

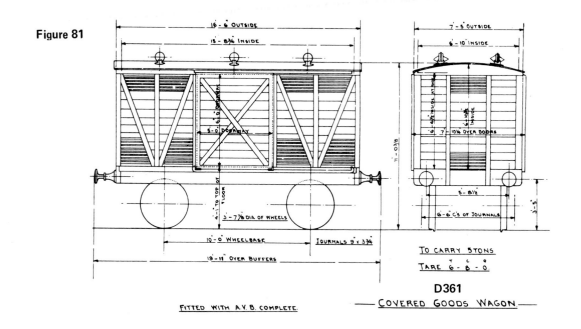

FITTED WITH A.V.B. COMPLETE.

TO CARRY 5 TONS
TARE 6 - 8 - 0.

D361

— COVERED GOODS WAGON —

Figure 82

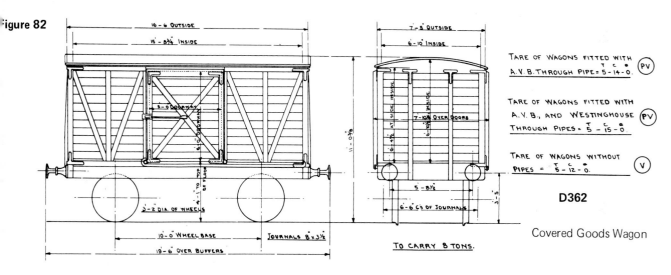

TO CARRY 8 TONS.

TARE OF WAGONS FITTED WITH
A.V.B. THROUGH PIPE = 5 - 14 - 0. (PV)

TARE OF WAGONS FITTED WITH
A.V.B., AND WESTINGHOUSE (PV)
THROUGH PIPES = 5 - 15 - 0.

TARE OF WAGONS WITHOUT
PIPES = 5 - 12 - 0. (V)

D362

Covered Goods Wagon

Figure 83

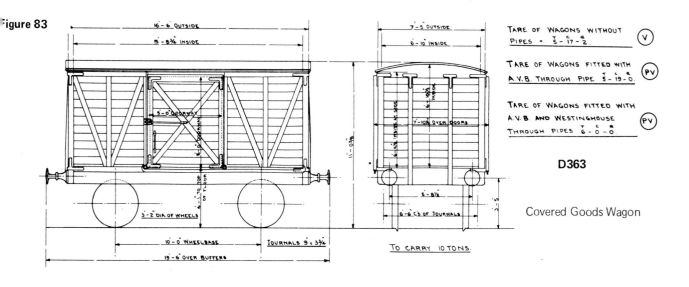

TO CARRY 10 TONS.

TARE OF WAGONS WITHOUT
PIPES = 5 - 17 - 2. (V)

TARE OF WAGONS FITTED WITH
A.V.B. THROUGH PIPE 5 - 19 - 0. (PV)

TARE OF WAGONS FITTED WITH
A.V.B. AND WESTINGHOUSE (PV)
THROUGH PIPES 6 - 0 - 0.

D363

Covered Goods Wagon

Figure 84

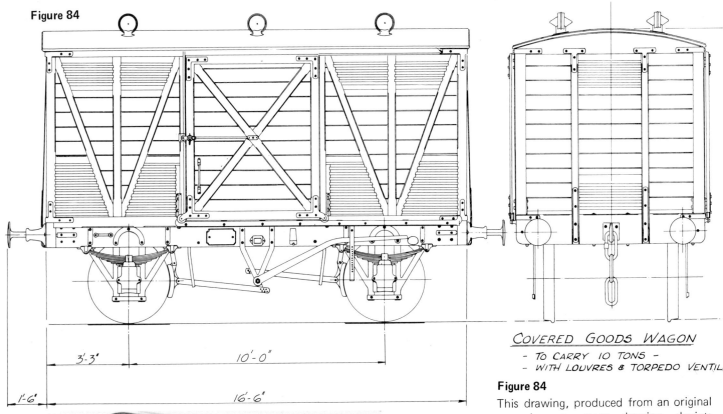

3'-3"   10'-0"

1'-6'

16'-6'

Plate 185

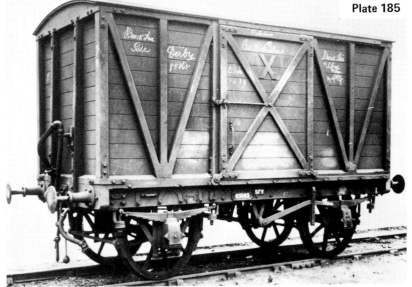

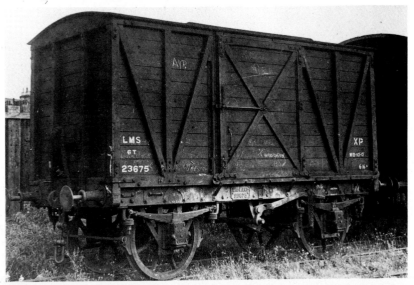

Plate 186

COVERED GOODS WAGON
- *TO CARRY 10 TONS -*
- *WITH LOUVRES & TORPEDO VENTIL*

Figure 84

This drawing, produced from an original general arrangement drawing, depicts D361, as originally built.

Drawing G.K. Fox

Plates 185 and 186 illustrate two vehicles to D360. **Plate 185** shows steam fitted van No. 85065. As mentioned in Chapter 9, these vans, coded SFV, were regarded as "Specials" by the Midland and were so recorded in the Special Wagon list (see Vol. II, chapter 9). However, the list of numbers totals 60, whereas the lot book suggests a total construction of 350 fitted vans and the author is unable to confirm if his interpretation of the lot book is correct. **Plate 186** which illustrates No. 23675 in L.M.S. livery, is a number not contained in the list of Special Wagons. Examination of these two plates reveals no "M.R." on 85065. The chalk dates suggest 1914. **Plate 186**, which shows No. 23675, is interesting and, when compared with 85065, shows a number of differences, i.e. no steam heating pipes, rain strip over door, L.M.S. axleboxes and different brake arrangement. The livery appears to be bauxite with the wartime size lettering.

When in L.M.S. grey livery, the 'X' was on the bottom half of the door, with the 'M' 12" high in place of the 'X'. The 'L' was where 'Derby' is chalked and the 'S' on the other side of the door. The location of the running number and tare weight is not known.

Photographs Plate 185 British Rail
Plate 186 A.G. Ellis

Plate 187

Plates **187—189** illustrate pre-1936, post-1936 and B.R. livery styles and conditions for D362 vans.

Plate 187 illustrates No. 4197 with oil axleboxes and both side brakes with no rainstrip, in L.M.S. grey.

Photograph Author's Collection

Plate 188 shows No. 90766 in bauxite photographed in April, 1939 (the 30.1.39 paint date is clearly visible.) The plate on the solebar appears to read "1907" which indicates lots 643 or 658.

Photograph A.E. West

Plate 189 is an example of lot 914 and was photographed in September, 1953. The body colour was light grey and, by this time, the vehicle must have been approaching the end of its active service in revenue traffic.

Photograph A.E. West

Plate 188

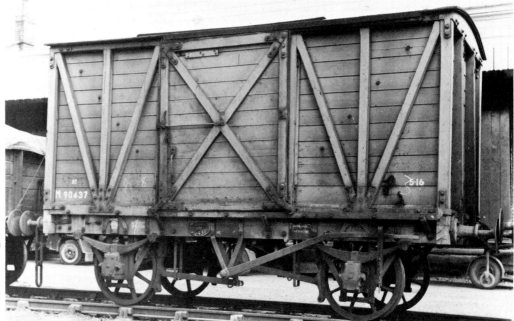

Plate 189

Plate 190

Plate

Plate 192

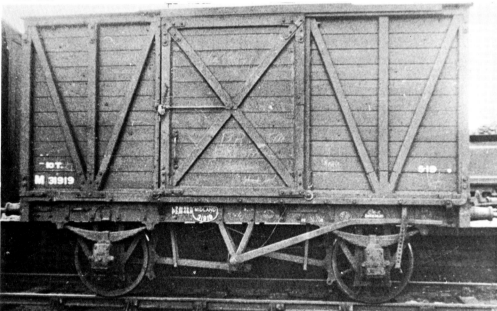

Plate 190 Covered goods wagon
3906 serves as the link between D362
D363. There is no sign of a capacit
this vehicle, hence the difficulty
deciding to which diagram it was
cated. Photographed in 1936, it cle
shows the pre-1936 L.M.S. livery styl

Photograph G.Y. Hemmin

Plate 191 illustrates No. 23318, ph
graphed in 1936 in newly painted
livery. This picture has been include
show the extra "L" section ironwor
the ends, the strengthening plate on
body near the top left hand side and
'Alpha Cement' notice on the door.
paint date on the solebar reads "6.5
but regrettably, its diagram alloca
cannot be confirmed, due to the imp
bility to read whether its capacity w
or 10 tons.

Photograph L.E. Cope

Plate 193

Plates 192 and 193 show the B.R.
running' livery for these two vehic
M31919 is 10T and, therefore, D3

Photograph Author's Collec

Plate 193 was photographed at Butte
and, in due course, will be restorec
Midland livery as No. 47961.

Photograph T.J. Edging

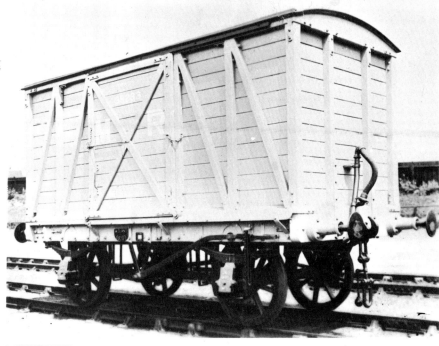

Plates 194 and 195 have been selected to illustrate the D363 variations to lots 938 and 941, which included both fitted and unfitted vehicles.

Plate 194 shows No. 68283 fitted with vacuum brakes or through pipes as built and clearly shows the Midland livery style in 1920.

Photograph British Rail

Plate 195 shows No. M111391 at Coalville in 1964 in B.R. 'unpainted' livery.

Photograph Author's Collection

Plate 196 Finally, illustrates the end of M2848 and has been selected to illustrate the alternate ironwork at the ends. Compare with the ironwork on the other Plates and the heavy "L" section on the end upright.

Photograph Author's Collection

TARE OF WAGON FITTED WITH A.V.B. THROUGH PIPE = 6-1-0 (PVV)

TARE OF WAGONS WITHOUT PIPES = 6-0-0 (VV)

D364
COVERED GOODS WAGON
AND FRUIT VAN

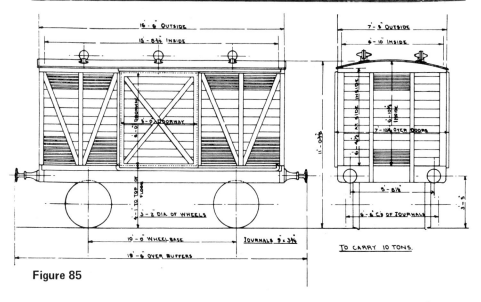

Figure 85

The remaining covered goods wagons, which were 16' 6" over headstocks and were largely designated for fruit traffic, are dealt with below. The principal visual difference, when compared with vans already described, was in the door design, with the earliest design being produced to drawing 1092 (Fig. 86.)

Diagram No.	Lot	Qty.	Date
D378	370	100	1896

Plate 197 This photograph of a covered goods wagon No. 15764 is something of a mystery and can only be an example of D378 which has received a new door and has been uprated to 10T capacity when converted from grease to oil axleboxes. Photographed in 1948.

Photograph H.C. Casserley

Plate 198 illustrates an ex-works photograph of No. 20639, an example of D378. Note the dual fitting of Vacuum and Westinghouse brake pipes and single side hand brake. The small "M.R." is interesting. Later it is felt that it would appear with the 'M' and the 'R' separated by the vertical bracing timber.

Photograph British Rail

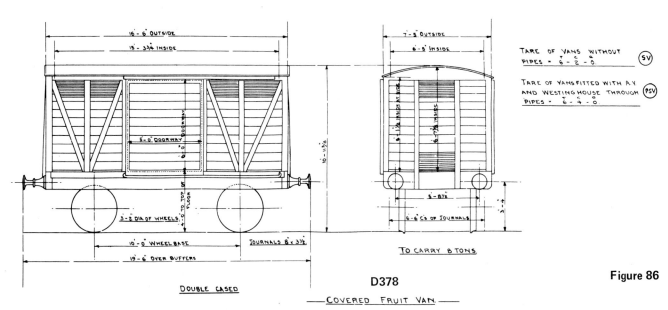

D378

— COVERED FRUIT VAN —

Figure 86

The next insertion in the lot book for vehicles allocated to fruit traffic in the wagon diagram book are:-

Diagram	Drawing No.	Lot	Qty.	Date	
D365 Figs. 87 & 89	2333	608	200	1905	Banana, louvres, torpedo vents, folding doors, double roof.
		649	100	1906	Banana, sliding doors, 75 folding doors, 25
			300		
D387 Fig. 88	2640	648	200	1906	Banana
D387 Fig. 90	3271	724	5	1909	Banana. Similar to Lot 649.
			205		

This totals 505 vehicles whose life in traffic would almost certainly be extinct by 1930 (D387) and 1939 for the remainder.

Of these 505 vehicles the 5 built to drawing 3271 are illustrated in Fig. No. 88, D387 and Fig. No. 90 which is a detailed drawing, together with **Plate No. 201**.

On 31 July, 1911 a banana van train was photographed near Hathersage and this train, hauled by a Class 3 No. 3797 is depicted in **Plate No. 199**. It appears to consist of flush-sided vans from lot 648 and includes the 5 vehicles of D387.

D365, Fig. No. 87, depicts a covered goods wagon which has folding doors and these are the 200 vehicles built to lot 608 and the 25 vehicles built to lot 649 with folding doors.

It is interesting to note that no diagram was issued to cover vehicles built to lot 648 (drawing 2640) and presumably, they were included under the D387 heading (see **Plate No. 202**), vehicle No. 117367. This plate illustrates banana van No. 117367 as originally constructed in 1906. A note on the drawing states:—

"Banana Van. Fitted with undergear to be run at Express Passenger Speed and with steam warming apparatus. To carry 6 tons by Passenger Train and 8 tons by Goods Train."

TARIFF VANS

The final design of 16' 6" covered goods wagon to be considered was in fact a tariff van. Regrettably, the author has never found any official document giving the Midland Railway Company's interpretation of 'Tariff'. However, it is felt that it referred to certain classes of merchandise which went by special traffic arrangements and for which higher freight rates applied. In some instances, this was under the control of the guard (see tariff brake vans, Chapter 11).

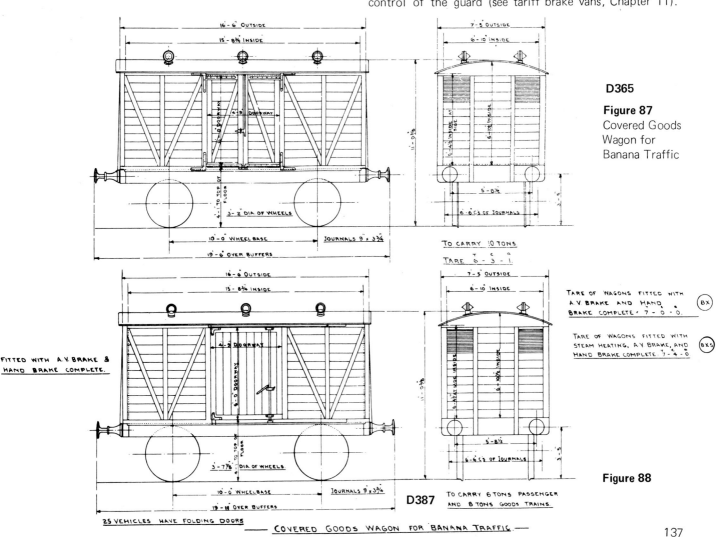

D365

Figure 87
Covered Goods Wagon for Banana Traffic

Figure 88

Plate 199 A specially posed pho graph of a banana van train near Hath sage on 31 July, 1911. The reason taking the photograph and selecting t location is unknown.

*Photograph British N

Plate 200 is the only known photograp of a vehicle to D361 where the number c be distinguished. On the original prir covered goods wagon No. 35324 w behind 4-4-0 No. 1740 and photographe at Cheltenham Lansdowne c1905.

Photograph B. Matthews Collecti

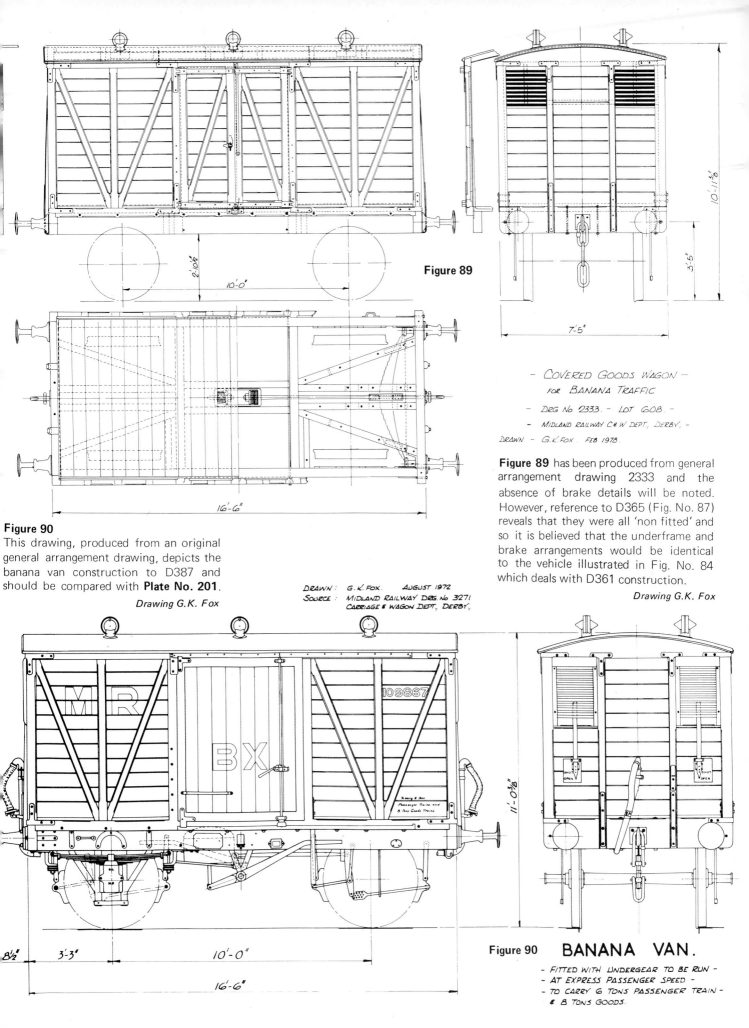

Figure 89

- COVERED GOODS WAGON -
- FOR BANANA TRAFFIC
- DRG No 2333. - LOT 608. -
- MIDLAND RAILWAY C & W DEPT., DERBY, -
DRAWN - G.K.FOX. FEB 1978.

Figure 89 has been produced from general arrangement drawing 2333 and the absence of brake details will be noted. However, reference to D365 (Fig. No. 87) reveals that they were all 'non fitted' and so it is believed that the underframe and brake arrangements would be identical to the vehicle illustrated in Fig. No. 84 which deals with D361 construction.

Drawing G.K. Fox

Figure 90

This drawing, produced from an original general arrangement drawing, depicts the banana van construction to D387 and should be compared with **Plate No. 201**.

Drawing G.K. Fox

DRAWN : G.K.FOX. AUGUST 1972
SOURCE : MIDLAND RAILWAY DRG. No 3271
CARRIAGE & WAGON DEPT., DERBY,

Figure 90 BANANA VAN.

- FITTED WITH UNDERGEAR TO BE RUN -
- AT EXPRESS PASSENGER SPEED -
- TO CARRY 6 TONS PASSENGER TRAIN -
  & 8 TONS GOODS.

Plate 201

Plate 202

The Midland built a number of tariff vans and the lot book contains the following entry:—

Drawing No.	Lot	Qty.	Date	Remarks
1239 (Fig. 91)	433	250	1898	50 piped with screw couplings and lamp

Very few pictures exist of these vans. One on which the number cannot be read, shows a larger 'M.R.' than that in **Plates 203 and 204**. The initials are 12" high and are each side of the vertical bracing. The only known picture in the L.M.S. period illustrates a hybrid vehicle which, although retaining the steps and general body style, has doors as per D362. Its number was 31597 and was branded 'Weighing Machine, Maintenance Tool Van'. The date was post-1936. It is therefore difficult to be precise about these vehicles. Almost certainly they would have been extinct, apart from any relegated to departmental stock, by c1930—5, but how long they were used for tariff traffic, the author is unable to state.

One possible clue to their use is to be found on a print taken from drawing 1239. On the left hand side reads the legend:—

'Bulk Grain Traffic
Avonmouth Docks to Workman Bros. Siding

Draycott Flour Mills
Coaley Junction

When empty return to Avonmouth Docks'.

However, there is no evidence of hopper bottom arrangements or a note of how many or which vans were so designated. This particular print does contain other interesting statements. One concerns the fitting of four rings and staples at each corner in September 1900 on four vans used between Bradford and Oxenhope. Another concerns the fitting of carriage door locks on 116096 in August, 1902 whilst a third statement is to the effect that louvres were to be fitted at each end at the side of the windows on wagons (not vans) Nos. 116156 and 116307. This was authorised in July 1910 and these louvres were to have shutters behind which folded back to the side of the wagon.

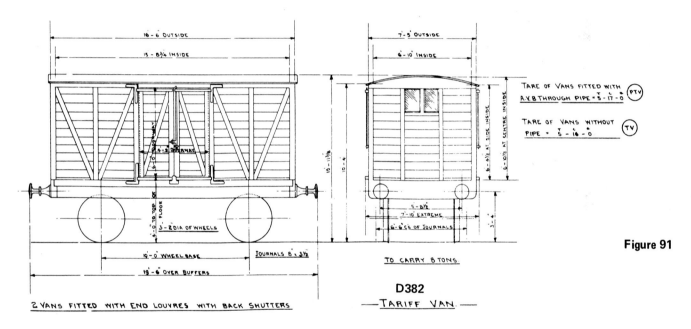

Figure 91

D382
—Tariff Van.—

◄ **Plate 201** shows an ex works photograph of No. 109858. This clearly illustrates D387 and attention is drawn to the 'passenger' style springs and large open spoke wheels. Note the extra packing pieces used with the buffer body to increase the length of the buffer.
Photograph British Rail

◄ **Plate 202** illustrates No. 117367 as built— an example of lot 648 allocated to D387. This clearly demonstrates that diagrams could cover vehicles which agreed with the dimensions but which visually were very different. Compare with **Plate 201**
Photograph British Rail

Running Numbers

D360	23675 (6.16) see Volume II Chapter 9 for the S.F.V.
D361	35364
D362	4197, 57471, (5.18), 8780 (5.19), 8940 (6.2), 7325. 90437 (5.16), 90766 (5.17), 114351 (5.10.0)
D363	31919 (5.19), 32504 (6.12), 47961. (28705 through pipe). Either D362/D363, 3906, 22700, 23318 (6.10), 68283, 4166, 92587.
D363	Lots 938/941, 2948 (5.18), 48595, 48604 (6.3.), 68283, 111391.
D364	Not known.
D365	Not known.
D378	20639 (6.1.2), 20850, 28850.
D382	116096, 116156, 116204 (5.12), 116240 (5.16.0), 116307.
D387	109858 (6.18.2), 117367 (Lot 648).

Plate 203 shows tariff van No. 116240 in ex-works livery. Unfortunately, the glass plate from which this print was made was damaged but attention is drawn to the legend on the bottom right hand corner of the vehicle which reads "For Tariff only, Return immediately to Bradford". Attention is drawn to the one side brake, together with the steps for loading and unloading away from the platforms. Note also the end windows to give light inside the vehicle.

Photograph British Rail

Plate 204 shows the 'no brake side' of No. 116204. On this vehicle the instructions were that it should be returned to Derby.

Photograph Author's Collection

17' 6" COVERED GOODS WAGONS

Two diagrams were issued to cover these final M.R. designs and the first drawing was No. 3557. The lot book records:—

Drawing No.	Lot	Qty.	Date	
3557	778	200	1911	Steel U/F, Steel framed body.
	786	100	1911	Unfitted
	822	200	1913	10T (Renewals)
Total		500		

These were followed by vehicles built to drawings 5098 and 5512 as below:—

Drawing No.	Lot	Qty.	Date		
5098	945	100	1920	10T	only difference was in axlebox size. W12 Lot 955, W7 Lot 970
	955	50	1920	12T	
	970	150	1921	10T	
5512	994	200	1922	12T	(also drawing 5098)
Total		500			

Examples of earliest vehicles would have lasted until nationalisation and the final lots would have run until c1960 or even later.

Comparison of the diagrams shows that D633 (Fig. 92) has 3' 7⅜" diameter wheels and was fully fitted, whilst D664 (Fig. 93) was only equipped with hand brakes. In addition, some of the D633 vehicles were equipped with steam heating pipes, thus enabling them to be run in passenger trains coupled next to the locomotive, and still allowing the train steam heating to operate. Unfortunately, the author cannot confirm how many were equipped with the various brakes, nevertheless, it is felt that all of the vehicles built to drawings 5098 and 5512 were not fitted together with the 100 constructed to lot 786. Those built to lot 778 were fitted but a question mark must exist about lot 882, although it is believed that they were unfitted.

This would mean that D633 referred to lot 778 with the remainder allocated to D664. Naturally, the vehicles built to lot 994 would never have run in Midland livery and some doubt must exist about their final appearance. L.M.S. diagram 1664 is identical to M.R. diagram 664, except that the L.M.S. diagram has a 9' 0" wheelbase, and the Midland vehicles have a 10' 0" wheelbase and the diagonal bracing at the left hand side is reversed. On the Midland vehicles, it runs up from the bottom left hand corner whilst, on the L.M.S. diagram, it runs down from the top left hand corner.

Before leaving these vehicles, attention must be drawn to the grain hopper version and **Plates 209** and **210** illustrate No. 88609. It is possible that these vehicles were all or part of lot 994 and that drawing 5098 refers to the hopper arrangements. The author has no knowledge of a Midland diagram and certainly no L.M.S. diagram exists. It is equally possible that some vehicles were converted, but the exact number involved in grain traffic is not known.

Known Running Numbers

D633   89451, 112423 (7.12.3)
D664   26223 (6.16) 35036 (7.1.)
Grain Hopper 88609.

Plate 205 illustrates No. 112423 in original Midland Railway condition. Comparison with **Plate 206** (which shows No. 89451 in August, 1946) reveals different wheels, modifications to the end panels and extra ironwork at the bottom corners.

Photograph British Rail Plate 205
Author's Collection, Plate 206

143

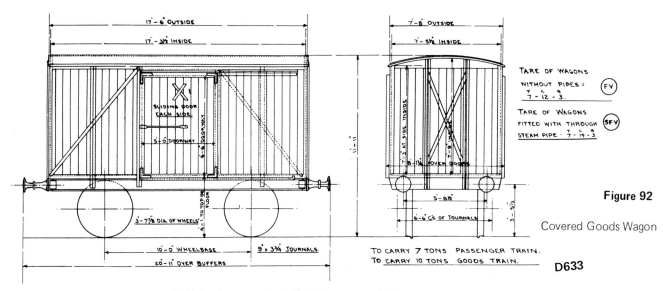

TARE OF WAGONS
WITHOUT PIPES:
T C q
7 - 12 - 3.   FV

TARE OF WAGONS
FITTED WITH THROUGH   SFV
STEAM PIPE T - C - q - 14 - 3.

Figure 92

Covered Goods Wagon

D633

TO CARRY 7 TONS PASSENGER TRAIN.
TO CARRY 10 TONS GOODS TRAIN.

FITTED WITH A.V.B AND
HAND BRAKE COMPLETE.

Plate 206

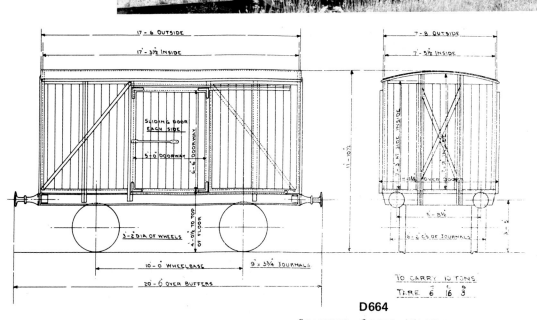

Figure 93

D664

COVERED GOODS WAGON

144

Plate 207

Plate 207 shows No. 26223 as running in October, 1939. It is presumed the livery was bauxite, the position of the numbers suggest this but it is possible that this wagon was painted grey and lettered in the post-1936 style, before the adoption of bauxite for the body colour.

Photograph A.E. West

Plate 208 illustrates No. M35036 in B.R. condition.

Photograph Author's Collection

Plates 209 and **210** show grain hopper wagon No. 88609, as running in July 1963 at Avonmouth and owned by the Port of Bristol Authority.

Photograph C.M. Strevens

Plate 209

Plate 208

Plate 210

Plate 211 illustrates meat van No. 7825 of lot 32 built in 1879. Compare with **Plate 212** which shows meat van No. 114128 of lot 305, which was built in 1892 and described in the lot book as 'lot 32 with detail alterations'. These variations include through brake pipe, cast iron not wooden brake blocks, short not long brake handle, second, not first, style of numberplate. One presumes that the ladder is on the other end of 7825; however, on the original print, the ice box covers seem to be lower on 114128, which has a handrail at the body corner—this may well also be on the hidden corner of 7825. The door-stop is different, so is the livery. Three link couplings replace five link. Note also the stirrup at the left hand end of No. 114128, 10A axleboxes on the later van, 8A on the earlier vehicle. All summed-up in the lot book as 'detail alterations'.

Photographs Both Plates
British Rail

Chapter 6 Vans for Special Traffic

This section deals with all the covered goods vans not included in the previous chapter—with the exception of those vehicles used to carry livestock, which will be found in Chapter 7, and this chapter includes the following types:—

Diagrams 370, 372, 374, 395. Refrigerator Meat Vans.
Figs. 95, 96, 97, 98
Diagrams 379, 396   Meat Vans Figs. 94, 99
Diagrams 384, 385   Gunpowder Vans Figs. 100, 101
Diagrams 368, 369   Covered Van for carrying motor cars
Figs. 102, 103
Diagram 833 Ventilated Van for carrying motor cars, etc.
Fig. 104
Diagram 367 Van for carrying road vehicles   Fig. 106
Diagrams 731, 834 Weighing Machine, Adjusting Van
Figs. 107, 108
No Diagram   Yeast Van Plate 240
No Diagram   Engineers Dept. Van Plate 241

It will be seen in Chapter 9 that the Midland Railway classified gunpowder vans, and some motor car vans which are dealt with in this chapter, as Specials. Other covered vehicles regarded as Specials were steam fitted vans, recorded in Chapter 5, and calf vans, recorded in Chapter 7 but the author's separation is believed to be more logical, in grouping the various types of vehicles in the above manner, rather than placing them all in Chapter 9.

Refrigerator Meat Vans Figure 95   (Page 150)

The Midland lot book records this sequence of construction:—

Diagram	Drawing No.	Lot	Qty.	Date	
D370	419	32	20	1879	
		305	30	1892	(as lot 32 with detail alterations)
		333	51	1894	As lot 305
Total			101		

Meat Vans Figure 94   (Page 148)

Diagram	Drawing No.	Lot	Qty.	Date	
D379	508	57	13	1881	Passenger Livery Meat Vans Nos. 13 & 61—72
		274	20	1891	Meat Vans with automatic vacuum brake & fish truck couplings
Total			33		

Diagram	Drawing No.	Lot	Qty.	Date	
D379	568	81	20	1882	Probably numbered 35450—69. Meat Vans to work in Goods Trains
		215	20	1888	Meat vans to work in Goods Trains.
		275	30	1891	Meat vans to work in Goods Trains. Fitted with automatic vacuum brake and fish truck couplings
		371	100	1896	50 piped, 50 fitted.
Total			170		

The passenger meat vans of lot 57 are not included in the December 1905 valuation list and must be presumed scrapped by that date and, by 1910, the withdrawal of lot 81 had commenced with all the vehicles, probably being withdrawn about that time. The exact date of withdrawal is not known but it is believed that, by c1925, lots 215/274—5/371 would have been replaced in traffic as meat vans. Whether these vehicles would have been regarded as 'life expired' or whether they would have been transferred to other traffics, is not known. Certainly, lot 371 which were about 25 years old, could have been considered still serviceable, but no pictures of this stock in L.M.S. livery have been recorded so the exact date of the end of their life in service is open to question.

Plate 212

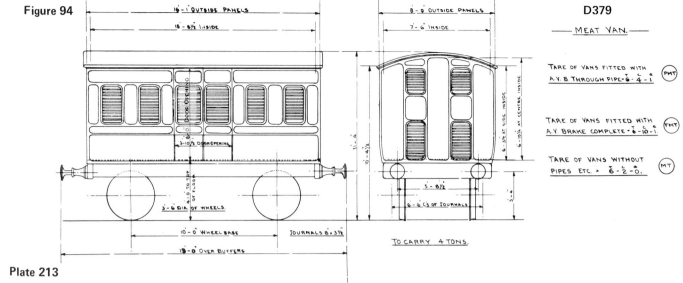

Figure 94

15-1 OUTSIDE PANELS
15-6½ INSIDE
DOOR OPENING
5-10½ DOOR OPENING
3-6 DIA OF WHEELS.
4-0 TO TOP OF FLOOR
10-0 WHEELBASE
JOURNALS 8 x 3½
15-0 OVER BUFFERS

8-9 OUTSIDE PANELS
7-6 INSIDE
11-4
10-4½
6-3½ AT SIDE INSIDE
6-10¼ AT CENTRE INSIDE
5-8½
6-6 C's OF JOURNALS
3-4

TO CARRY 4 TONS.

D379

MEAT VAN.

TARE OF VANS FITTED WITH
A.V.B. THROUGH PIPE - 6-4-1 (PMT)

TARE OF VANS FITTED WITH
A.V. BRAKE COMPLETE - 6-10-1 (FMT)

TARE OF VANS WITHOUT
PIPES ETC = 6-2-0. (MT)

Plate 213

Plate 213 illustrates meat van No. 62 as running in 1887 in red passenger livery. This plate, together with the other three pictures illustrating meat vans, have been chosen to show the differences between the various lots in respect of brake gear and pipes, footsteps and livery.

Photograph British Rail

Plate 214 shows meat van No. 35468 of lot 81 as running in 1887 in grey livery. Compare with **Plate 213** to see the difference between passenger and goods meat vans.

Photograph British Rail

Plate 214

Plate 215 is a picture of meat van No. 5817 of lot 371. By now this 'Goods Meat Van' in grey livery has the large 'M.R.' on the bodyside, a handbrake on one side only but is fitted with vacuum brakes and could be run in passenger trains—note the lamp brackets.

Photograph British Rail

Plate 216 illustrates meat van No. 35463 towards the end of its life, and is the only picture known to the author of one of these vehicles in service where its number can be clearly seen, they usually appear in background views which will be used in later volumes—note no steps or brakes on this side of the vehicle.

Photograph Author's Collection

Figure 95

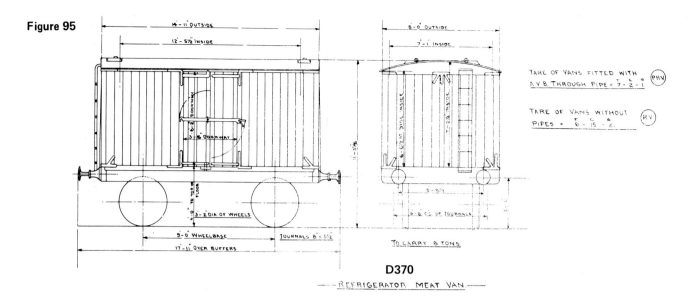

D370
REFRIGERATOR MEAT VAN

Figure 96

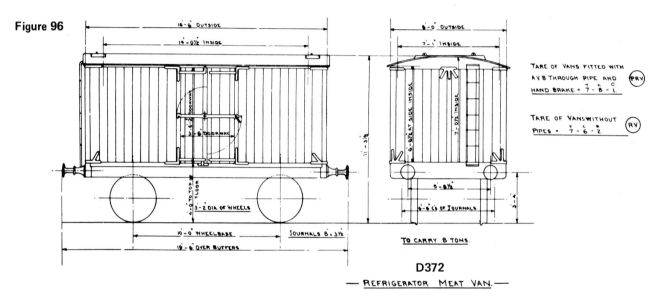

D372
REFRIGERATOR MEAT VAN.

In 1896 further meat van construction commenced and the details are as below:—

D372	Refrigerator Meat Van		Fig. 96	
Drawing No.	Lot	Qty.	Date	
1102	372	100	1896	50 piped

Two years later, a new drawing was issued for what was basically the same design but with larger wheels, with an emphasis on passenger train working.

D374	Refrigerator Meat Van		Fig. 97	
Drawing No.	Lot	Qty.	Date	
1271	444	110	1898	fitted for passenger trains
	480	100	1900	as lot 444 with detail alterations
Total		210		

Unfortunately, only one picture is known to exist, see **Plate No. 217** and so the detail alterations are not known. These vehicles to both D372 and 374 probably lasted only until the late 1920's before being scrapped and replaced by new L.M.S. standard construction.

In 1910, further vehicles were built to two different designs, as below:—

D395	Refrigerator Meat Van		Fig. 98	
Drawing No.	Lot	Qty.	Date	
3331	743	7	1910	Refrigerator
	771	5	1911	
	777	20	1911	Refrigerator Meat
Total		32		

D396	Refrigerator Meat Van		Fig. 99	
Drawing No.	Lot	Qty.	Date	
4320	744	3	1910	

Figure 97

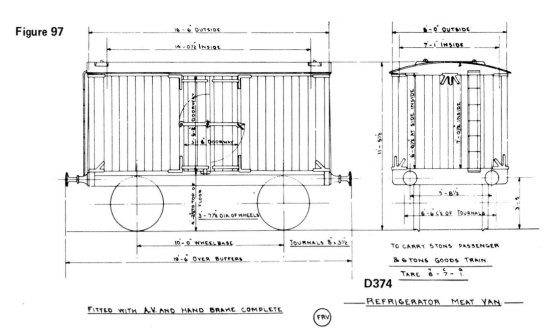

16'-6" OUTSIDE
14'-0½" INSIDE

8'-0" OUTSIDE
7'-1" INSIDE

3'-6" DOORWAY

11'-5½"

6'-6½" AT SIDE INSIDE
7'-0½" INSIDE

4'-10" TOP OF FLOOR
3'-7½" DIA. OF WHEELS

5'-8½"
6'-6" C's OF JOURNALS
3'-5"

10'-0" WHEELBASE
JOURNALS 8 x 3½

19'-6" OVER BUFFERS

TO CARRY 5 TONS PASSENGER
& 6 TONS GOODS TRAIN.
TARE 8 - 7 - 1

FITTED WITH A.V. AND HAND BRAKE COMPLETE

(FRV)

D374

— REFRIGERATOR MEAT VAN —

Figure 98

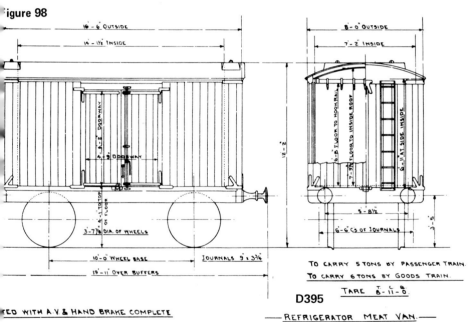

16'-6" OUTSIDE
14'-1½" INSIDE

8'-0" OUTSIDE
7'-2" INSIDE

4'-2" DOORWAY

3'-9" DOORWAY

12'-2"

6'-8" FLOOR TO HOOK RAIL
7'-9¾" FLOOR TO INSIDE ROOF
6'-11" AT SIDE INSIDE

4'-10" TOP OF FLOOR
3'-7⅞" DIA. OF WHEELS

5'-8½"
6'-6" C's OF JOURNALS
3'-5"

10'-0" WHEEL BASE
JOURNALS 9 x 3¾

19'-11" OVER BUFFERS

TO CARRY 5 TONS BY PASSENGER TRAIN.
TO CARRY 6 TONS BY GOODS TRAIN.
TARE 8 - 11 - 0

FITTED WITH A.V. & HAND BRAKE COMPLETE

D395

— REFRIGERATOR MEAT VAN —

Plate 217 illustrates refrigerator meat van No. 23553 of lot 372 in original condition and attention is drawn to the light livery, black ironwork and the black shading to the right and below the lettering.

Photograph British Rail

Plate 217

Plate 218 illustrates refrigerator meat van No. 2422 as built, and again attention is drawn to the black ironwork and shading to the lettering, together with the legend 'To carry 5 tons on Passenger Trains' and 'To carry 6 tons by Goods Trains'. Figure 98.

Photograph British Rail

Almost certainly these vehicles were considered as replacement for D379 vehicles, referred to earlier in the chapter and it is interesting to see that three vehicles only were built as meat vans and allocated a new diagram number.

A further quantity was built in 1915 and 1918, as below, but no trace of a new diagram has been found.

Drawing No.	Lot	Qty.	Date	
4320	902	20	1915	Refrigerator Meat
	930	20	1918	
Total		40		

The only photographs which have been recorded are similar to that illustrated in **Plate 220** and this background view illustrates a van similar in roof profile to D395, but with strapping identical to the vehicles built for overseas service illustrated in Chapter 1 page 45, **Plate No. 47**. It seems likely that these 40 vehicles were of this type and **Plate 220** illustrates their L.M.S. livery. A drawing of No. 114970 of this class appeared in the Railway Modeller, (page 372) December 1975. The 1930's saw many changes in the transport of meat and the rapid introduction of containers by the L.M.S. probably rendered these Midland vans extinct by c1935.

The only known running numbers appear in the Plates, no other information being available.

Figure 99

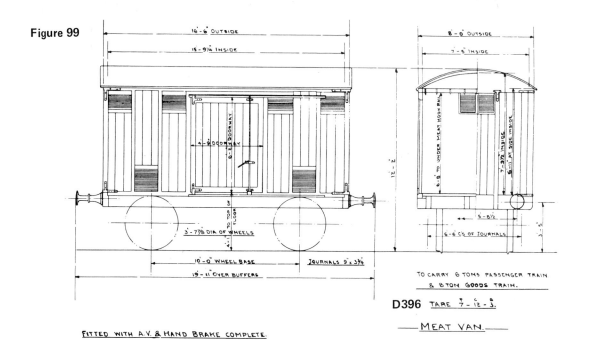

FITTED WITH A.V. & HAND BRAKE COMPLETE.

TO CARRY 6 TONS PASSENGER TRAIN
& 8 TON GOODS TRAIN.

D396 TARE 7 - 12 - 3.

MEAT VAN.

Plate 219 illustrates meat van No. 35464 in original condition. Unlike D395, D396 vehicles were allowed to carry 8 tons in goods trains and were branded 'To be returned to Carlisle'.

Photograph British Rail

Plate 220 illustrates what is believed to be an example of a vehicle built to drawing 4320 in L.M.S. livery. Regrettably, the running number cannot be established.

Photograph A.G. Ellis

Plate 220a. This background view sh No. 59165 while on the same orig picture, of which this is a part, sh van Nos. 38143 and 73935 which identical except for the lack of diag bracing.

Photograph British

GUNPOWDER VANS D384 & D385

Figures 100 & 101

The Midland only built 20 gunpowder vans but, in 1912, when they purchased the LTSR, their stock was increased by a further 25—see Chapter 13, Volume II. Due to Midland practice of regarding these vehicles as specials, all the running numbers are recorded upon the diagrams and the lot book records this information.

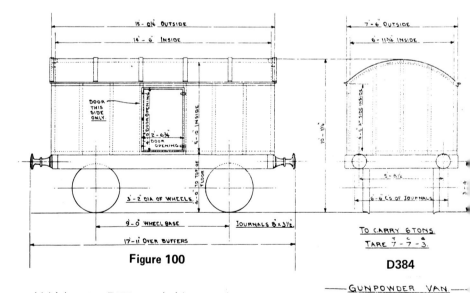

Figure 100

Vehicles to D385 probably ran in traffic until c1940 and Plates 221—223 illustrate both diagrams. Regrettably, no photographs are known to exist showing Midland vans carrying L.M.S. livery but it is felt they would have followed standard L.M.S. practice.

D384

— GUNPOWDER VAN

NUMBERS
522
1679
1898
7599
18208

Diagram 384		Gunpowder Van	
Drawing No.	Lot	Qty.	Date
528	68	2	1881
	179	2	1887
	328	1	1893
Total		5	

Probably extinct by c1925

Diagram 385		Gunpowder Van	
Drawing No.	Lot	Qty.	Date
2109	583	15	1904

Plate 221 illustrates van No. 1679 in original condition. The body appears to be light grey with a slate grey roof. Built in 1881, the only evidence of ownership is the numberplate, and the legend on the left hand end reads "Powder Van, when empty to be returned to Derby". Note the very small doorway 2'6" x 4'0" but on one side of the van only. Finally, attention is drawn to the fact that it is an iron body on a wooden underframe. Note the iron stops at the end to prevent the body moving on the frame.

Photograph British Rail

Figure 101

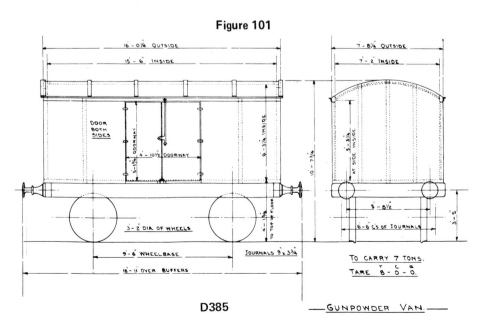

NUMBERS	
30804	32510
30861	32583
31623	32845
31710	33463
31860	34057
32127	34110
32215	34604
32470	

D385 — GUNPOWDER VAN. —

TO CARRY 7 TONS.
TARE 8 - 0 - 0.

Plate 222

Plate 222 illustrates van No. 32215. This 1904 batch was equipped with much larger doors, which were located on both sides of the van. Note the brake gear. At the time No. 32215 was photographed, it was equipped with brakes on both sides but the handles were at the same end, practice which became illegal and, in due course, all vehicles had to be altered so that, when viewed side-on, the brake handle had to be at the right hand end of the vehicle. Compare with **Plate 223** van No. 32510. Note the black background on the number and notice plates on this vehicle.

Both Photographs British Rail

Plate 223

The above description has been selected by the author to describe this style of vehicle which, in modern parlance would probably be called a C.C.T. or P.M.V. and during the period 1904—15, a total of 146 vans were constructed as below:—

Diagram	Drawing No.	Lot	Qty.	Date
368	2022	582	4	1904
368	1830/2191	596	4	1904
414	2415	609	25	1905
414A		699	1	1908 For
				M & G.S.W.
414A		705	1	1908
369	2549	642	12	1906
369		668	20	1907
369		725	3	1909
414A	3393	755	12	1910
414A	3727	806	12	1912
833	4213	893	52	1914
Total			146	

However, not all these vehicles were considered freight stock and those built to diagram 414 and 414A were regarded as passenger stock. Diagram 414 were square light and 414A were round light. Overall length was 31' 0". An example of lot 609 is illustrated in **Plate 225.**

The Midland regarded this type of freight vehicle as a 'special' and a number of them are recorded in the list of special wagons (see Fig. No. 126, Volume II, Chapter 9) however, not all appear to have been so classified.

D368 **Motor Car Van** **Fig. 102**

Running Nos. on diagram. In 1928 they were renumbered 4434/8253/64/5 and, in 1933, they were renumbered 37298—37301 and were withdrawn between 1939—48. This renumbering followed the decision by the L.M.S., in 1928, to transfer these vehicles to non-passenger coaching stock and, in consequence, they were painted crimson lake and carried passenger livery. The renumbering in 1933 followed the total renumbering of all coaching stock by the L.M.S. when the previous random numbers were consolidated into identifiable blocks (see **Plate 224.**)

Similar to
D357 **Motor Car Van** **See Fig. 75** **Page 124**

These four vehicles, part of lot 596, were in effect D357 but with end doors. Their running numbers are not known and, since they were not duplicated, it is presumed they were not a success. It is possible they reverted to normal freight duties.

D369 **Motor Car Van** **Fig. 103**

Original numbers are on the diagram. In 1928 they were renumbered 4479, 8204—8/10—3/6. 4503, 8217/9/20/22—4/7/8/30—4/6—8. 8218/26/29 in order of the date of construction and, in 1933, they were renumbered 37302—32. Some were withdrawn before 1933 but the general date of withdrawal was during the mid-late 1940's (see **Plate 226**).

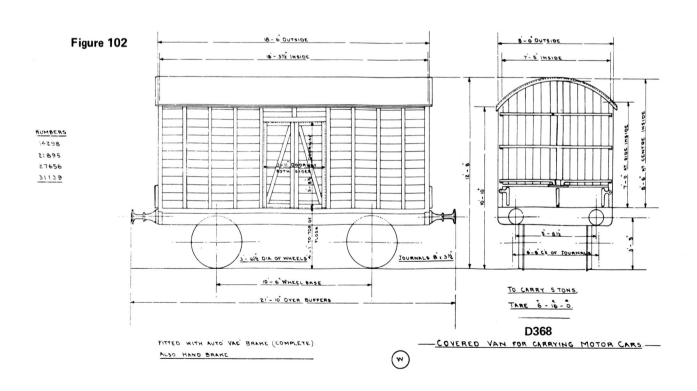

Figure 102

NUMBERS
14298
21895
27656
31129

FITTED WITH AUTO VAC BRAKE (COMPLETE)
ALSO HAND BRAKE

D368
COVERED VAN FOR CARRYING MOTOR CARS

Figure 103

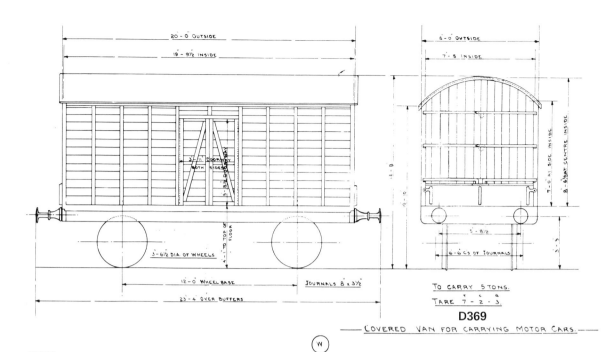

D369

COVERED VAN FOR CARRYING MOTOR CARS.

FITTED WITH AUTO VAC BRAKE (COMPLETE).
ALSO HAND BRAKE.

Plate 224 illustrates D368 motor car van No. 14298 in original condition and livery. Note the large diameter spoked wheels and lamp irons for use when running at the rear of passenger trains.

Photograph British Rail

Plate 224

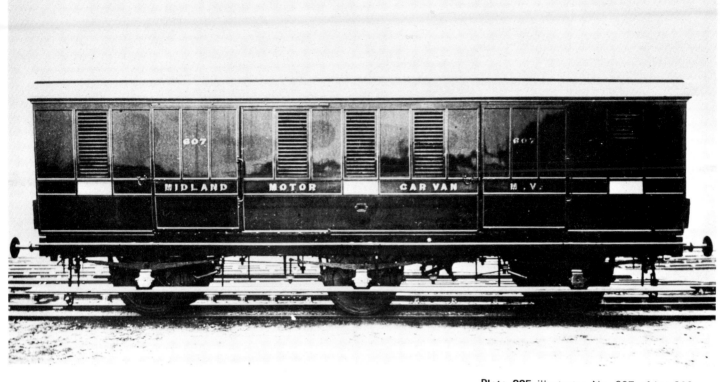

Plate 225 illustrates No. 607 of lot 609, a passenger rated motor car van.

Photograph British Rail

Plate 226 Loading a Rolls Royce Silver Ghost chassis into No. 1688 of D369 at Derby. This photograph clearly illustrates the end loading technique employed.

Photograph British Rail

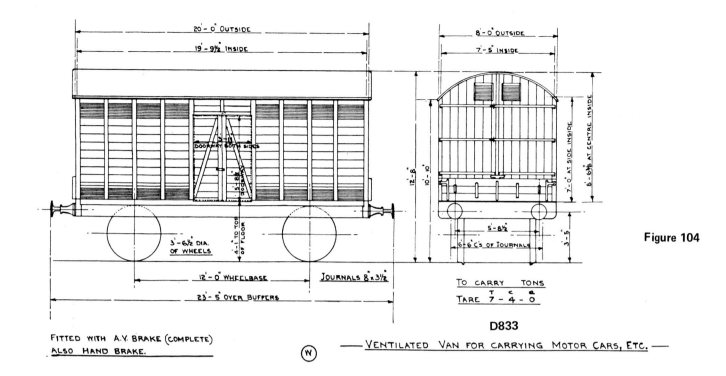

FITTED WITH A.V. BRAKE (COMPLETE)
ALSO HAND BRAKE.

Figure 104

D833

—— VENTILATED VAN FOR CARRYING MOTOR CARS, ETC. ——

**D833   Ventilated Van for Carrying   Figs. 104 & 105
            Motor Cars etc.**

This was the final design of 20' 0" long van and, unlike the previous vehicles, these were classified as 'ventilated'. They do not feature on the list of special vehicles (Fig. No. 126, Vol. II) and some of their original running numbers were 1734 / 1901 / 3120 / 3732 / 7338 / 7509 / 8379 / 8812. 17059 / 17798 / 22296 / 26481 / 26533 / 26570 / 114156 / 63 / 82 / 114257 / 8 / 26433. 35583 / 80091 / 80345 / 80551 / 63 / 114221 / 114339 in building sequence. In 1928 they were renumbered 4501, 8200–2 / 14 / 5 / 25 / 35 / 40 – 8 / 50 – 2. 8254 – 63 / 6 – 77 / 79 – 87. The earliest withdrawal was 1947 and the type was finally withdrawn from service in 1959. See **Plate Nos. 227/228.**

Figure 105 is a drawing of D833 in original condition but, as noted on the drawing, the end louvres were later removed whilst in service (see also **Plate Nos. 227/228.**)

Drawing by T.W. Bourne

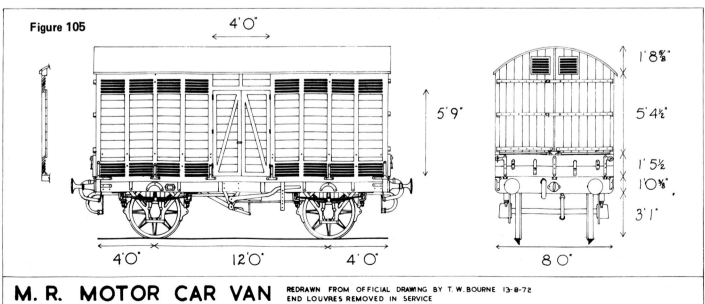

Figure 105

M. R. MOTOR CAR VAN   REDRAWN FROM OFFICIAL DRAWING BY T.W. BOURNE 13·8·72
                                           END LOUVRES REMOVED IN SERVICE

Plate 227 illustrates motor car van No. 26548 of D833 in original condition. Note the original open spoked wheels when compared with Plate No. 228.

Photograph British Rail

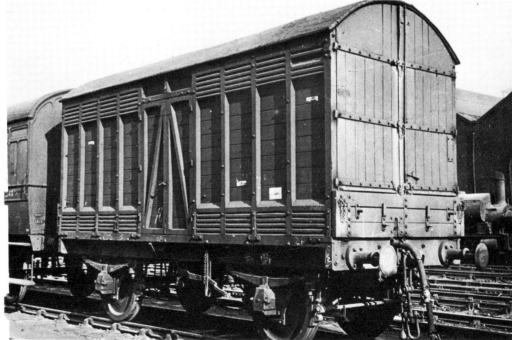

Plate 228 illustrates an unidentified example of D833 in service and branded 'P.M.V.'

Photograph Author's Collection

In addition to this 1904—15 construction, two other vehicles were built, rated as freight stock, and classified within the 'Road Vehicle' category.

D367   Van for carrying Road Vehicles   Fig. 106

Running Nos. in diagram.

Drawing No.	Qty.	Lot	Date
750	2	206	1888

Almost certainly withdrawn before 1928, possibly even before 1923, their original description was 'covered goods wagon' (see Chapter 5, page No. 121).

Plate 229 illustrates No. 742 in original condition but in photographic livery—note method of painting wheels and brake gear.

Photograph British Rail

Finally, although never classified as freight stock and therefore not given Midland freight diagrams were a number of covered carriage trucks and the opportunity has been taken to include some illustrations if only to again underline how fine the line was between various types of vehicles when their classifications were determined (see **Plates 230—232**.)

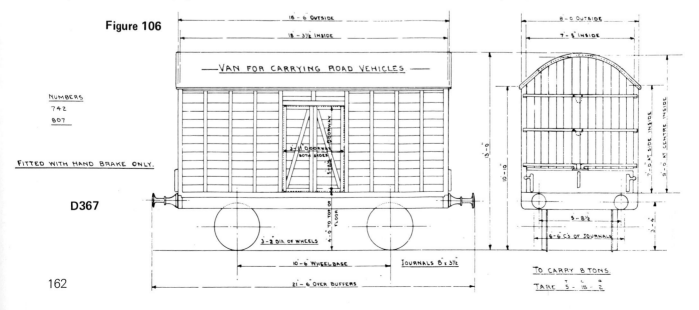

Figure 106

NUMBERS
742
807

FITTED WITH HAND BRAKE ONLY.

D367

VAN FOR CARRYING ROAD VEHICLES

18 - 6 OUTSIDE
18 - 3½ INSIDE

3 - 11 DOORWAY BOTH SIDES

3 - 2 DIA OF WHEELS
10 - 6 WHEELBASE
JOURNALS 8 x 3½
21 - 6 OVER BUFFERS

8 - 0 OUTSIDE
7 - 5 INSIDE

13 - 0
10 - 0

5 - 8½
6 - 6 C3 OF JOURNALS

TO CARRY 8 TONS
TARE 5 - 18 - 2

Plate 230

Plate 230 is No. 217, a covered carriage truck of 1875 in original condition.

Plate 231 is No. 90, a covered carriage truck from lot 59 of 1881, while **Plate No. 232** illustrates No. 74, a covered carriage truck of lot 121 from 1886. However, these vehicles more probably belong to the history of Midland passenger rated vehicles rather than a volume dealing with freight vehicles.

Plates 230—232 British Rail

Plate 231

Plate 232

163

SIGNAL DEPT. & WEIGHING MACHINE ADJUSTING VANS

Within the realms of vans for special traffic, we have to consider two departmental types of vehicles, which are very similar in outward appearance, namely Signal and Telegraph and weighing machine adjusting vans. Only the latter were given diagrams, Nos. 731 and 834, with the latter apparently only having one vehicle allocated. The lot book records as below:—

Vans for Signal Dept.

Drawing No.	Lot	Qty.	Date
26	55	2	1880

Weighing Machine and Adjusting Vans

Drawing No.	Lot	Qty.	Date	
26	21	1	1878	
701	180	6	1887	
	245	4	1890	Vans for Signal & Weighing Machine Depts. One for weighing Dept. to have internal fittings
	313	1	1893	As lot 245
	421	1	1897	Van for Signal Dept. as lot 245 but 3″ longer to suit standard underframe for covered Goods.
	468	2	1899	As lot 421 for Signal Dept.
	541	1	1902	As lot 313 but 3″ longer Weighing Dept.
	793	1	1912	Weighing Dept.
	811	1	1912	Weighing Dept. as lot 793
1507	515	1	1901	Weighing Machine test wagon 16 tons.
3882	829	1	1913	Weighing Machine
	868	1	1914	Weighing Machine as lot 829
	872	1	1914	Weighing Machine as lot 868
	897	3	1915	Weighing Machine as lot 872
	898	3	1915	Signal Dept. Repairing Van (no internal fittings)
Total		28		

It will be noted that a total of 30 vans were produced to four drawings; one was a special which meant three drawings for twenty nine vehicles. From these thirty it appears that eleven went to the Signal Dept. and nineteen to the Weighing Dept.

From examination of the diagrams (Figs. 107 & 109) it will be noted that there is a double door on one side and a single door on the other. This was common to all drawings, except perhaps for drawing 1507 but no pictures are known to exist for this vehicle. Diagram 731 (Fig. 107) appears to refer to vans built to drawings 26 and 701, whilst diagram 834 (Fig. 109) refers to drawing 3882 and reference to the Plates will cover the detail differences. Naturally the diagram for drawing 701 refers to the final size but **Plate 233** illustrates the original construction. Vehicles of this type were long lived and could have lasted 50 years before withdrawal.

Figure 107

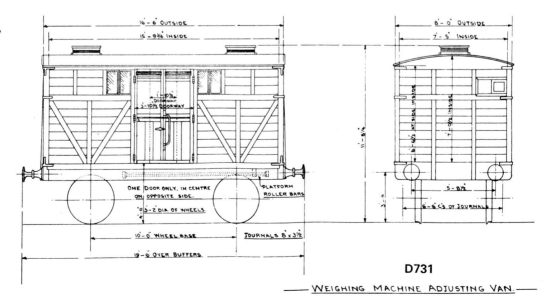

D731

— WEIGHING MACHINE ADJUSTING VAN. —

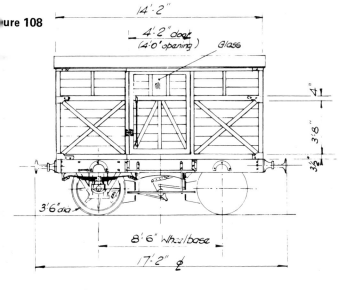

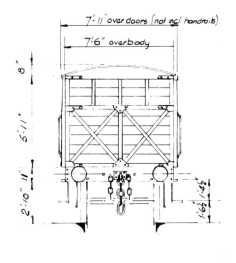

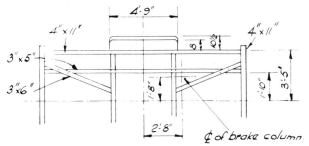

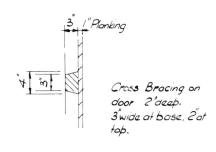

Cross Bracing on
door 2' deep.
3" wide at base, 2" at
top.

Framing of Body
Corner Posts 4½" × 4"
Rest 4" × 4" unless stated
otherwise.

Door framing 3" × 3"
unless otherwise stated.

Midland Railway
Tranship Van.
built by Metropolitan R.C.&W.Ltd.
c.1865.

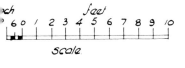

scale.

Tranship Van

This drawing produced from a Metropolitan R.C. & W. Co. Ltd. original depicts a 'Signal Dept. or Weighing Machine Van' nevertheless the original drawing records the description, 'Tranship Van'. It is interesting to note that the brake is inside the vehicle and it is possible that the original 'Tranship Van' design was later adopted for departmental use as depicted in **Plates 233 and 234**.

Drawing G.N.I. Ibbott

Plate 233 illustrates No. 31584 of lot 55 and the similarity to the Metropolitan drawing in Fig. No. 108 should be noted. The other vehicle of lot 55 was probably No. 31585 (see **Plate No. 235**).

Photograph British Rail

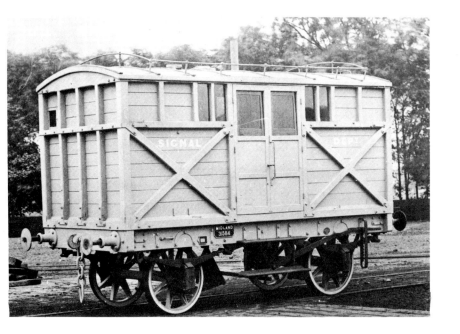

Plate 234 illustrates weighing machine adjusting van No. 18 of lot 180, as built, but in photographic livery.

Photograph British Rail

Plates 235 and 236 illustrate No. 31585 and it seems logical to assume that this was probably a replacement for the other vehicle of lot 55. However, the author cannot be certain.

Photograph Author's Collection

Plate 235

Plate 236

There is a contradiction in as much as the diagram notes show running number 7479, probably built to lot 829, but no doubt the construction was identical to lots 868/72/97/98. A total of eight more vans was built to the same design (see **Plate 239**).

Plate 237 illustrates the second No. 31584 as running in 1934. On a time in service basis one would expect this replacement to be lot 898, but grease axleboxes suggest earlier construction. Unfortunately, the author is unable to provide any further information.

Photograph R.E. Lacy

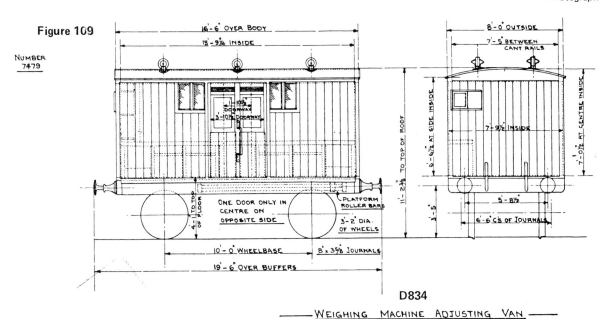

Figure 109

NUMBER 7479

16'-6" OVER BODY
15'-9¼" INSIDE
1'-10½" DOORWAY
3'-10½" DOORWAY
ONE DOOR ONLY IN CENTRE ON OPPOSITE SIDE
PLATFORM ROLLER BARS
3'-2" DIA. OF WHEELS
4'-1" TO TOP OF FLOOR
11'-2⅜" TO TOP OF ROOF
10'-0" WHEELBASE
8" x 3⅝" JOURNALS
19'-6" OVER BUFFERS

8'-0" OUTSIDE
7'-5" BETWEEN CANT RAILS
6'-6½" AT SIDE INSIDE
7'-9½" AT CENTRE INSIDE
7'-9½" INSIDE
3'-5"
5'-8½"
6'-6" C'S OF JOURNALS

D834
— WEIGHING MACHINE ADJUSTING VAN —

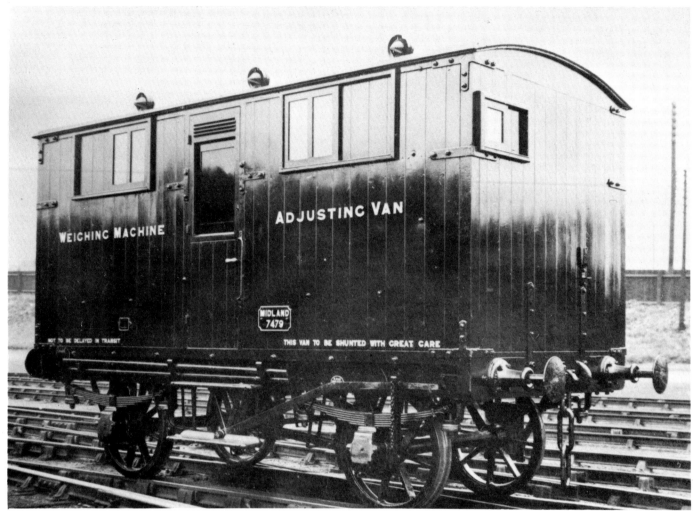

Plate 238 illustrates weighing machine adjusting van No. 7479 in original condition, almost certainly being from lot 829. This vehicle appears to be painted red oxide or black, probably the former.

Photograph British Rail

Plate 239 illustrates No. M41644 in the early 1950's and, when compared with **Plate No. 238** clearly shows the different door arrangements which were a feature of these vehicles.

Photograph A. Dunbar

YEAST VANS
No Diagrams issued Plate 240

The picture of van No. 23029 appears to be a medium cattle wagon with extra louvres and the legend at the right hand end, 'To be Returned to Burton,' suggested some connection with the brewing industry. However, nothing is recorded in the lot book and so matters remained unanswered until the author examined 'Photographs of Midland Wagon Stock' (see Chapter 1 page 26). This revealed item 61 'Yeast Vans'—12 built in 1896, 16' 3'' over headstocks, 5.19.0 tare weight, to carry 8 tons. In the author's view, these twelve vans were conversions of 16' 3'' length medium cattle wagons, (diagram 293) which could explain the absence of a reference in the lot book. No further details are known about their life in traffic, workings or final withdrawal.

Photograph British Rail

Plate 240

ENGINEERS DEPT. VAN
No Diagram issued Plate 241

Plate 241

Even less is known about the department van illustrated in **Plate 241**. A number of interesting features can be seen, i.e. steel underframe, vacuum pipes, heavy duty buffers, all steel construction and a 'CCT' type roof profile. Regrettably, the author has not been able to locate anything recorded about this unusual vehicle.

Photograph British Rail

Midland Freight Trains ~ and so on to Volume 2